## Critical Acclaim for Books by Gen and Kelly Tanabe
### Authors of *Get into Any College, Get Free Cash for College* and *1001 Ways to Pay for College*

"Upbeat, well-organized and engaging, this comprehensive tool is an exceptional investment for the college-bound."

—PUBLISHERS WEEKLY

"Helps college applicants write better essays."

—THE DAILY NEWS

"Invaluable information."

—LEONARD BANKS, THE JOURNAL PRESS

"A present for anxious parents."

—MARY KAYE RITZ, THE HONOLULU ADVERTISER

"Helpful, well-organized guide, with copies of actual letters and essays and practical tips. A good resource for all students."

—KLIATT

"When you consider the costs of a four-year college or university education nowadays, think about forking out (the price) for this little gem written and produced by two who know."

—DON DENEVI, PALO ALTO DAILY NEWS

"What's even better than all the top-notch tips is that the book is written in a cool, conversational way."

—COLLEGE BOUND MAGAZINE

"Offers advice on writing a good entrance essay, taking exams and applying for scholarships, and other information on the college experience—start to finish."

—TOWN & COUNTRY MAGAZINE

"I recently applied to Cornell University. I read your book from cover to back, wrote an essay about 'Snorkeling in Okinawa' (which most people criticized), and got ACCEPTED to Cornell. Thank you very much for your help, and I'll be sure to refer this book to anyone applying to college."

"If you're struggling with your essays, the Tanabes offer some encouragement."

—COLLEGE BOUND MAGAZINE

"A 'must' for any prospective college student."

—MIDWEST BOOK REVIEW

"The Tanabes literally wrote the book on the topic."

—BULL & BEAR FINANCIAL REPORT

"Filled with student-tested strategies."

—PAM COSTA, SANTA CLARA VISION

"Actually shows you how to get into college."

—NEW JERSEY SPECTATOR LEADER

"Upbeat tone and clear, practical advice."

—BOOK NEWS

# 50 Successful
## UNIVERSITY
## OF CALIFORNIA
# Application
# Essays

Includes advice from University of Californa admissions officers and the 25 essay mistakes that guarantee failure

## GEN and KELLY TANABE

HARVARD GRADUATES AND AUTHORS OF
*50 Successful Ivy League Application Essays,*
*Accepted! 50 Successful College Admission Essays and*
*The Ultimate Scholarship Book*

*50 Successful University of California Application Essays*
By Gen and Kelly Tanabe

Published by SuperCollege, LLC
2713 Newlands Avenue
Belmont, CA 94002
www.supercollege.com

Credits: Cover: TLC Graphics, www.TLCGraphics.com. Design: Monica Thomas. Cover photo: © Panpan914 | Dreamstime.com.
Layout: The Roberts Group, www.editorialservice.com

Trademarks: All brand names, product names and services used in this book are trademarks, registered trademarks or tradenames of their respective holders. SuperCollege is not associated with any college, university, product or vendor. Disclaimers: The authors and publisher have used their best efforts in preparing this book. It is sold with the understanding that the authors and publisher are not rendering legal or other professional advice. The authors and publisher cannot be held responsible for any loss incurred as a result of specific decisions made by the reader. The authors and publisher make no representations or warranties with respect to the accuracy or completeness of the contents of the book and specifically disclaim any implied warranties or merchantability or fitness for a particular purpose. The accuracy and completeness of the information provided herein and the opinions stated herein are not guaranteed or warranted to produce any particular results. The authors and publisher specifically disclaim any responsibility for any liability, loss or risk, personal or otherwise, which is incurred as a consequence, directly or indirectly, from the use and application of any of the contents of this book.

ISBN13: 978-1-61760-031-9

Manufactured in the United States of America
10 9 8 7 6 5 4 3 2 1

# TABLE OF CONTENTS

# DEDICATION

To our readers—
we hope you achieve your dream!

# ACKNOWLEGMENTS

THIS BOOK WOULD NOT HAVE BEEN possible without the generous contributions of the University of California students who agreed to share their admissions essays and advice in order to help others who hope to follow in their footsteps.

We would also like to thank the former University of California admissions officers for spending the time to impart some of their knowledge to our readers: Jasmine Thompson, Kim Glenchur and Eddie LaMeire.

We would like to express our deepest appreciation to contributing writer Elizabeth Soltan.

Thanks also to Lynda McGee, college counselor at Downtown Magnets High School, for connecting us to many of the students.

Special thanks to Alice Hu, Laura Malkiewich and Mark Fujiwara.

# 1

# 25 ESSAY MISTAKES THAT GUARANTEE FAILURE

FOR EVERY OPEN SLOT AT UC Berkeley or UCLA, there are about five eager applicants vying for it–and you're one of them. On paper, most applicants appear very similar. All are well-qualified academically with high grades and test scores and solid involvement in extracurricular activities.

Imagine the admissions officer who must choose which of these well-deserving applications to accept. How will he or she make the decision? Very often, the essay makes a difference. The essay is the one chance for you to share a piece of yourself that is not encapsulated in the dry numbers and scores of the application. It is your opportunity to demonstrate why you'd be a perfect fit at the college, how you'd contribute to the student body and why the college should accept you over those other four applicants.

The essay is also the one part of your application that you have complete control over. You can write it the night before it's due and turn in a piece that is half-baked, or you can spend a little time on the essay and turn in one that can set you apart from the competition.

The truth is that you don't have to be a good writer to create a successful admissions essay. Nor do you need to have survived a life-changing event or won a Nobel Prize. Writing a successful admissions essay for the UC schools is actually much simpler.

The secret is that any topic can be a winner but it all depends on your approach. If you spend the time to analyze your subject and can convey with words that quality of thought that is unique to you, you'll have a powerful essay. It doesn't have to be beautifully written or crafted as the next great American novel. At its core the essay is not a "writing test." It's a "thinking test." So you do need to spend the time to make sure that your thoughts are conveyed correctly on paper. It may not be pretty writing but it has to be clear.

So how do you do this? While we can give you tips and pointers (which is what you'll read in the analysis section following every essay) the best method is to learn by example. You need to see what a successful end product looks like. While there is no single way to produce a winning essay, as you will read, there are some traits that successful essays share. You'll learn what these are by reading the examples in this book as well as the interviews with admissions officers. Then you can write a successful essay that is based on your own unique experiences, world view, way of thinking and personal style.

Why are admissions essays so important to getting into the UC schools? At their most basic level, essays help admissions officers to understand who you are. While grades, test scores and academic performance can give the admissions officers an estimate on how prepared you are to handle the academic rigors of college, the essay offers the only way they can judge how your background, talents, experience and personal strengths come together to make you the best candidate for their school. For you, the applicant, the admissions essays offer the best opportunity to share who you are beyond the dry stats of your academic record. It's kind of amazing actually. You start with a blank sheet of paper and through careful selection, analysis and writing, you create a picture of yourself that impresses the admissions officers and makes them want to have you attend their school.

Ultimately, this book is designed to help you create a successful essay that gets you accepted. It will guide you toward writing that essay by sharing with you the successes of others who have written to gain admission to UC schools.

If you're like most students, you would like to know the magic formula for writing an admissions essay. Although we would love to be able to tell you, unfortunately, no such formula exists. Writing is so individual and the options so limitless, that it's impossible to develop a combination that will work for *every* essay. However, this doesn't mean that we're going to send you off with laptop in hand, without some guidance. Throughout this book you are going to see the "right way" to do things. So we thought it would be useful to start off with a few common mistakes that other students have made. You'll want to avoid these. In fact, some of these mistakes are so bad that they will almost guarantee that your essay will fail. So avoid these at all costs!

1. **Trying to be someone else.** This may sound very obvious, and well, it is. But you'd be surprised at how many students don't heed this simple piece of advice. A lot of students think that they need to be who the admissions officers want them to be; in reality, the admissions officers want you to be you. They aren't looking for the perfect student who is committed to every subject area, volunteers wholeheartedly for every cause, plays multiple sports with aptitude and has no faults. Instead, they want to learn about the true you. Present yourself in an honest way, and you will find it much easier to write an essay about your genuine thoughts and feelings.

2. **Choosing a topic that sounds good but that you don't care about.** Many students think that colleges seek students who have performed a lot of community service, and it is true that colleges value contributions to your community. However, this doesn't mean that you must write about community service, especially when it's not something that has played a major role for you. The same holds true for any other topic. It's critical that you select a topic that's meaningful to you because you will be able to write about the topic in a complete and personal way.

3. **Not thinking before writing.** You should spend as much time thinking about what you will write as actually putting words on paper. This will help you weed out the topics that just don't go anywhere, determine which topic has the greatest pull for you

and figure out exactly what you want to say. It can help to talk yourself through your essay aloud or discuss your thoughts with a parent, teacher or friend. The other person may see an angle or a flaw that you do not.

4. **Not answering the question.** While this seems simple enough, many students simply do not heed this. The advice is especially pertinent for those who recycle essays. We highly recommend recycling because it saves you time to write one essay that you use for many colleges, but the caveat is that you need to edit the essay so that it answers the question being asked. It turns admissions officers off when students submit an essay, even a well-written one, that doesn't answer the question. They think that the students either aren't serious enough about the college to submit an essay that has been specifically written or at least edited for that college, or that they just don't follow directions. Either way, that's not the impression you want to give.

5. **Not sharing something about yourself.** As you know, the main purpose of the admissions essay is to impart something about yourself that's not found in the application. Still, many students forget this, especially when writing about a topic such as a person they'd like to meet or a favorite book or piece of literature. In these cases, they may write so much about why they admire the person or the plot of the book that they forget to show the connection to themselves. Always ask yourself if you are letting the admissions officers know something about yourself through your essay.

6. **Forgetting who your readers are.** Naturally you speak differently to your friends than your teachers, and when it comes to the essay, some applicants essentially address the admissions officers with a too-friendly high five instead of a handshake. In other words, it's important to be yourself in the essay, but you should remember that the admissions officers are adults not peers. The essay should be comfortable but not too informal. Remember that adults generally have a more conservative view of what's funny and what's appropriate. At the same time, admissions officers are generally not senior citizens. They are typically younger, sometimes recent college graduates, and more in tune

with teenage interests and popular culture than you may think. The best way to make sure you're hitting the right tone is to ask an adult to read your essay and give you feedback.

7. **Tackling too much of your life.** Because the essay offers a few hundred words to write about an aspect of your life, some students think that they need to cram in as many aspects of their life as possible. This is not the approach we recommend. An essay of 500 to 800 words doesn't afford you the space to write about your 10 greatest accomplishments since birth or about everything that you did during your three-week summer program in Europe. Rather, the space can probably fit one or two accomplishments or one or two experiences from the summer program. Instead of trying to share your whole life, share what we call a slice of your life. By doing so, you will give your essay focus and you will have the space to cover the topic in greater depth.

8. **Having a boring introduction.** Students have started their essays by repeating the question asked and even stating their names. This does little to grab the attention of the admissions officers. Sure, they'll read the whole essay, but it always helps to have a good start. Think about how you can describe a situation that you were in, convey something that you strongly believe in or share an anecdote that might not be expected. An introduction won't make or break your essay, but it can start you off in the right direction.

9. **Latching on to an issue that you don't really care about.** One of the prompts for the Common Application is, "Discuss some issue of personal, local, national or international concern and its importance to you." The key to answering this question is to carefully think about these words: "its importance to you." This is what students most often overlook. They select an issue and write about the issue itself, but they don't really explain why it is important to them or how they see themselves making an impact. If you write about an issue, be sure to pick one that is truly meaningful to you and that you know something about. You'll probably score extra kudos if you can describe how you have done something related to the issue.

10. **Resorting to gimmicks.** Applicants have been known to enclose a shoe with their essays along with a note that reads, "Now I have one foot in the door." They have also printed their essays in different fonts and colors, sent gifts or food and even included mood music that's meant to set the mood while the admissions officer reads the essay. A few students have even sent cash! While gimmicks like this may grab some attention, they don't do much to further the applicants, especially those few who've sent money, a definite no-no. It's true that you want for your essay to stand out but not in a way in which the admissions officer thinks that you are inappropriate or just plain silly. If you have an idea for something creative, run it by a teacher or counselor to see what he or she thinks first.

11. **Trying to make too many points.** It's better to have a single, well thought-out message in your essay than many incomplete ones. Focusing allows you to go into depth into a specific topic and make a strong case for your position. Write persuasively. You can use examples to illustrate your point.

12. **Not being specific.** If you think about some of the best stories you've been told, the ones that you remember the most are probably filled with details. The storyteller may have conveyed what he or she thought, felt, heard or saw. From the information imparted, you may have felt like you were there or you may have developed a mental image of the situation. This is precisely the experience that you would like the admissions officers to have when reading your essay. The key to being memorable is providing as many details as possible. What thoughts were going through your mind? What did you see or hear? What were you feeling during the time? Details help bring the admissions officers into your mind to feel your story.

13. **Crossing the line.** Some students take to heart the advice to share something about themselves, but they end up sharing too much. They think that they must be so revealing that they use their essay to admit to something that they would never have confessed otherwise. There have been students who have written about getting drunk, feeling suicidal or pulling pranks on their teachers. It's possible that in the right context, these topics might

work. For example, if the pranks were lighthearted and their teachers had a good sense of humor about them, that's acceptable. But for the most part, these kinds of topics are highly risky. The best way to determine if you've crossed the line is to share your idea with a couple of adults and get their reactions.

14. **Repeating what's in the application form.** The essay is not the application form, and it is not a resume. In other words, the essay is the best opportunity that you'll have to either delve into something you wrote in the application form or to expound on something new that doesn't really fit on the application form. It doesn't help you to regurgitate what's already on the application form.

15. **Not having a connection with the application form.** While you don't want to repeat information from the application form verbatim in your essay, it's usually a good idea to have some continuity between the form and your essay. If you write an essay about how your greatest passion in life is playing the piano and how you spend 10 hours a week practicing, this hobby should be mentioned in the application form along with any performances you've given or awards you've won. It doesn't make sense to write about how you love an activity in the essay and then to have no mention of it in the application form. Remember that the admissions officers are looking at your application in its entirety, and they should have a complete and cohesive image of you through all the pieces, which include the application form, essay, transcript, recommendations and interview.

16. **Not going deep enough.** One of the best pieces of advice that we give students is to keep asking, "Why?" As an example, let's say that you are writing an essay on organizing a canned food drive. Ask yourself why you wanted to do this. Your answer is that you wanted to help the homeless. Ask yourself why this was important to you. Your answer is that you imagined your family in this situation. You would greatly appreciate if others showed compassion and helped you. Why else? Because you wanted to gain hands-on experience as a leader. The point of this exercise is to realize that it's not enough to just state the facts or tell what happened, that you organized a canned food drive. What makes

an essay truly compelling is explaining the "why." You want the readers of your essay to understand your motivation. Keep asking yourself why until you have analyzed the situation as fully as possible. The answers you come up with are what will make your essay stronger.

17. **Not getting any feedback.** Practically every article that you read in a magazine, book or newspaper or on the Internet has been edited. The reason is that writing should not be an isolated experience. You may know exactly what you want to convey in your own mind, but when you put it on paper, it may not come out as clearly as it was in your mind. It helps to get feedback. Ask parents, teachers or even friends to read and comment on your essay. They can help you identify what can be edited out, what needs to be explained better or how you can improve your work.

18. **Getting too much feedback.** Asking one or two people for feedback on your essay is probably enough. If you ask more than that, you may lose the focus of your writing. Having too many editors dilutes your work because everyone has a different opinion. If you try to incorporate all of the opinions, your essay will no longer sound like you.

19. **Trying to be extraordinarily different.** There are some people who are extraordinarily different, but the truth is that most of us aren't. What's more important than conveying yourself as the most unique person at your school is that you demonstrate self-analysis, growth or insight.

20. **Ruling out common topics.** There are topics that admissions officers see over and over again such as your identity, your relationship with your family, extracurricular activities and the Big Game. While these topics are very common, it doesn't mean that you shouldn't write about them. Your topic is not as important as what you say about it. For example, many students choose to write about their moms or dads. A parent can be one of the most influential persons in a student's life, and it makes sense that this would be the topic of many students' essays. So don't rule out Mom or Dad, but do rule out writing about Mom or Dad in the way that every other person will write. Explain how your dad

made banana pancakes every morning and what that taught you about family, or how your mom almost got into a fight with another mom who made a racist comment. Make a common topic uncommon by personalizing it.

21. **Forcing humor.** You've probably seen at least one sitcom on TV or one monologue by Conan O'Brien or David Letterman with a joke that fell flat. Maybe you groaned at the TV or gave it an un-amused expression. Keep in mind that the jokes on TV are written by professional writers who earn large salaries to be funny. Now, remember that the great majority of us are not headed down this career path. What this means is that you shouldn't force humor into your essay. If you're a funny writer, then by all means, inject some humor. Just be sure to ask an adult or two to read the essay to see if they agree with you that it is funny. If you're not humorous, then it's okay. You don't need to force it.

22. **Writing the essay the night before it's due.** Almost every student has done it—waited until the last minute to write a paper or do a project. Sometimes it comes out all right, but sometimes not so much. It is not wise to procrastinate when it comes to writing a college admissions essay. It takes time. Even if you are able to write an essay the night before it's due, it's still better not to. The best essays marinate. Their authors write, take some time away from it and then return to it later with a fresh mind.

23. **Failing the thumb test.** As you are writing your essay, place your thumb over your name. Could you put another name at the top because it could be an essay written by many other students? Or is the essay personal to you so that basically yours is the only name that could be at the top? If you fail the thumb test, it's time to rethink the topic or your approach to it. You want your essay to be unique to you.

24. **Forgetting to proofread.** Some students put the wrong college name in their essays, a mistake that could easily be avoided by proofreading. Many more students have spelling, grammatical or punctuation errors. While these types of errors usually aren't completely detrimental, they can be distracting at best and be signs to the admissions officers that you're careless and not

serious about their college at worst. Avoid this by not only using your computer's spell check but by asking someone else to help proofread your essay. Twice is better.

25.   **Not writing to the specific college.** In addition to learning about you, the admissions officers also hope to learn how you would fit in at the University of California schools. You don't need to explicitly list reasons why the UC schools are the best place for you, but it helps to keep in the back of your mind how you would contribute to the environment.

26.   **Not spending time on the rest of your application.** Remember that the essay is one piece of the application. It can certainly help your chances of being accepted, but you need to have everything else in place as well. Sure, it takes time to work on the application form, recommendation letters and interviews, but you are taking actions now that will affect the next four years of your life and beyond. It's worth the effort.

## How to Use This Book

Now that you have a clear of idea of the mistakes to avoid in your essay, it's time to get some advice on what you *should do*. Let's go directly to the source—University of California admissions officers. In the next chapter, former University of California admissions officers share what they seek in applicants and give you tips on how to make the strongest impression on them.

Then, see what makes a solid essay through the essays themselves. Of course, the point is not to copy these essays. It's to gain inspiration. It's to see what's worked in the past and to get your creativity flowing so that you can formulate in your mind how you can best approach your topic.

We've analyzed each of the essays too. You'll see that even essays written by students accepted at one of the premier colleges in the country are not perfect and have room for improvement. You'll also see the strengths of the essays so that you can make sure to incorporate similar characteristics.

By learning through example, you can create the most compelling and persuasive essay possible. You'll know what not to do, you'll understand what the admissions officers want and, perhaps most importantly, you'll be inspired to write your own successful UC admissions essay.

# UNIVERSITY OF CALIFORNIA ADMISSIONS OFFICER Q&A

**EDDIE LAMEIRE**
Former Reader, UC San Diego
Former Associate Director, UC San Diego Cal-SOAP College Outreach Program
Head Consultant, LaMeire College Consulting

**Q:** Can you give students an idea of what happens to their applications and essays after they are received by the college?

**A:** I had experience with two entirely different offices, and the reads had little in common. The distinctions are what would be expected between private and public schools considering the sizes of their respective applicant pools.

When I began in admissions, I worked at a private university, Loyola University, and the attention given to the students was extensive. Each piece of the application was processed as it arrived, and we had (for that time) a sophisticated system of recording the components.

As an Admissions Counselor/Senior Counselor, I traveled, ultimately allowing me to have the first review of the student's file. I knew the differences in academic rigor between, say, Albuquerque Academy and Albuquerque High School, which the senior staff didn't. This is pretty standard for most admissions offices: the regional officer gets first crack at the application.

I would go through the app, calculate the GPA (we recalculated entirely, which was exhausting), record the test scores and make note of any salient issues: ethnic minority status; prospective major (business majors specifically were held to higher standards); exemplary extracurricular activities and significant life experiences. I'd print a report, make a recommendation for admission or denial and move the application up the chain of command. If the next reader (usually an Associate Director) disagreed with my suggestion, we'd debate the applicant's merits and her potential "fit" for the school. After, if we were still at loggerheads, we'd appeal to a Director.

My experience with UC was different, and it makes sense why. At Loyola, we had about 3,400 applicants for a freshman class of about 850. When I was with UCSD, the school was looking at over 40,000 applicants! So, the care that I took with students at Loyola was almost entirely absent at UC. Of course, UC doesn't do interviews or look at letters of recommendation, but even considering this, the process was truly spartan. I need to be clear, though: I last worked with UC in 2005, and things have changed considerably since then. Furthermore, I was at one of nine UCs. But, this gives you a window into how the process generally works at larger schools. Welcome to the assembly line!

So, to continue, I was presented weekly with a box of applications, typically to be read by the end of the following week. Applications were accompanied by a score sheet (known as an OSCAR). Thankfully, GPA and SAT recording was done by the processors, and my job was to go through different parts of the application and tally up non-academic "points." We issued points for everything from low-income and single-parent home status all the way through number of volunteer hours and level of awards.

My read of the application had little to do with "fit," and the time that I spent on the applications gave me only the faintest idea of the student's personality. If the applicant had a compelling personal story, this would certainly help them. However, I was largely combing through the app to see if there was anything that I could possibly give points for—academic, demographic and otherwise—from the essays (specifically) as well as the application in general.

**Q: What specific advice do you have for the freshman applicant prompt?**

*Describe the world you come from—for example, your family, community or school—and tell us how your world has shaped your dreams and aspirations.*

**A:** The applicant should treat this prompt as a story arc that spans the breadth of his (relevant) life. In a nutshell, this is a brief autobiography that should show the applicant's development and maturation, as well as how that development and maturation have led to his desires for the future. I encourage students to use this essay as the longer of the two essays—usually about 600-650 words. There's so much to review in an "autobiography" that it typically warrants a good amount of space.

It's always preferable if the student can refer to both personal and academic factors here and show how they intertwine. For instance, not only should a potential Spanish major indicate his academic background in Spanish, but he should also give an idea why he's interested in the language. A trip to Mexico as a child? A sculpture of Don Quixote in the family living room? A mother who's a diplomat? It's like the antique market: personal stories add value.

The dreams and aspirations should be reasonable, but they should also be approached with a degree of passion. Even during my time with the point system, legitimate, intense passion (backed up by evidence) could have made a difference in the final application score.

**Q: What specific advice do you have for the second prompt for all applicants?**

*Tell us about a personal quality, talent, accomplishment, contribution or experience that is important to you. What about this quality or accomplishment makes you proud and how does it relate to the person you are?*

**A:** For this one, I'll usually recommend using about 350 words or so. It's more of a "slice of life" essay, which doesn't need the story arc demanded by the first prompt. The most effective way of doing this is to identify a quality the student is proud of; illustrate it through an example and extrapolate it to other parts of her life.

Typically, if a student has a particularly significant accomplishment—big science fair win, Girl Scout Silver Award, internship—I recommend that she go into it here. There still needs to be some character development and maturation in this essay; the essay is not meant to be a resume dump.

**Q: What are some of the most common mistakes that students make when writing their essays?**

**A:** People will mention everything from citing the name of another school to committing grammar errors, but these really aren't common or all that egregious. The most common problem—as well as one that can be a killer for both UC and private schools—is treating the essay as a heavily annotated resume.

Again, even at UCSD we wanted to see more than pieces of data. We wanted to see passion and commitment. There's a place for a resume on the application: the accomplishments/awards/volunteer section, not the essay.

Additional stylistic issues are standard: Lack of detail, telling instead of showing and the like. However, the big one is dumping data rather than showing who you are as a person. Accomplishments are good, but universities are in the business of admitting people, not CVs.

**Q: Can you think of an example or two of when an applicant wrote about an ordinary topic in an extraordinary way?**

**A:** The best instance I have of this is a student who wrote about his passion for engineering . . . but within the context of his mechanical creations that drove his neighbor crazy. The centerpiece of the essay was a "potato cannon" made from vacuum tubes other random household items, and it fired vegetables all over the neighborhood. I loved the approach, which I still remember.

Another example, albeit from when I was at Loyola, was a student who wrote about his pride in his Muslim heritage . . . just after the September 11, 2001, attacks. The approach was so earnest and gutsy that I still consider it among the better essays I've read—for the chance the student took, if nothing else.

**Q: Are there any topics or approaches to topics that students shouldn't write about?**

**A:** The "extreme" essays are always risky. If a student has had discipline problems, issues with drugs or general behavioral issues, they need to convincingly show that they've overcome them. I only recommend approaching the essay in this way when a student has confronted the issue early enough in their high school career to permit the reader to believe that they've gotten beyond it. If, for instance, a student gets involved with a gang during junior year, it's not too believable that he's done with it by application time during his senior year. Only the filter of time can separate students from a past that they want to get beyond.

**Q: How important is the essay? In your experience, has it ever made the difference between a student being accepted or not?**

**A:** The essay is hugely important, although its importance ranges from campus to campus. As large and bureaucratic as UC might be, they are still looking at personal history, at persistence and at talent. I have seen students with a 3.6 UC GPA admitted to Berkeley because they had such unique and impressive stories. The essay is the only place to disclose this! Even when I was using the point system, the proper presentation of both personality and accomplishments often meant the difference between admission and denial.

**Q: Is there anything that a student might find surprising either about your selection process or about what you are looking for in the essays?**

**A:** When I was with UC, what even I found shocking was the speed with which I was able to read the applications. What the student spent months building I would rip through in less than five minutes. I needed to do this. I was largely paid for speed!

What I tell my students now—and what I've tried to emphasize here—is the need to balance detail of accomplishment with a story. I needed a story to keep my attention. But, without the appropriate level of detail, it was difficult for me to award points.

Of course, things are now different with the read, but I find that the same general advice works: Discuss what you've achieved, but do it in a way that allows you to look human and authentic.

> Eddie LaMeire has worked in admissions and outreach since the late 1990s, in public and private, large and small schools. He currently works as an independent college consultant in the Silicon Valley (www.lameirecollegeconsulting.com), working with students from the San Francisco Bay Area, Taiwan and China.

## JASMINE THOMPSON, MA
**Former Admissions Representative, UC Davis**
**Education Consultant**

**Q: Can you give students an idea of what happens to their applications and essays after they are received by the college?**

**A:** In a major system like the University of California, students must complete two major phases during the admissions process. The first phase is system wide eligibility, which is calculated using the student's GPA and standardized test scores (see link below). If a student is deemed UC eligible, the application is allowed to proceed in the admissions process. The subsequent phase is selection, a complex analysis of the student's academic rigor, extracurricular activities and life experiences. Multiple admissions readers review applications to discourage bias and to ensure a holistic analysis.

http://admission.universityofcalifornia.edu/freshman/california-residents/admissions-index/index.html

**Q: What specific advice do you have for the freshman applicant prompt?**

*Describe the world you come from—for example, your family, community or school—and tell us how your world has shaped your dreams and aspirations.*

**A:** Many students make the mistake of focusing on the object, person or organization and fail to depict the personal meaning, impact or expression. Students should provide background and content of their chosen topic and be sure to explain its impact on their life experience.

**Q: What specific advice do you have for the second prompt for all applicants?**

*Tell us about a personal quality, talent, accomplishment, contribution or experience that is important to you. What about this quality or accomplishment makes you proud and how does it relate to the person you are?*

**A:** Students should use this prompt to explore an activity or leadership role and find correlation to their intended major and/or career. Similar to the previous prompt, the intent of the personal statement is to display additional information that is limited or not found elsewhere in the application.

**Q: What are some of the most common mistakes that students make when writing their essays?**

**A:** The first common mistake is not answering the prompt questions or using the same essay from a different application without modification. The second common mistake is the misconception to "go from the heart string" without proper content or evidence. For instance, students will write about a family pet's illness or a common issue that has minimal impact (i.e. running out of gas or receiving a poor grade on a quiz). Students should express meaningful information that cannot be found in other areas of the application. Lastly, students should not exploit a situation for the illusion of an obstacle or struggle.

**Q: Can you think of an example or two of when an applicant wrote about an ordinary topic in an extraordinary way?**

**A:** Unfortunately, I cannot recall an essay that illustrated an ordinary topic in an ordinary fashion; the college-going culture in America has elevated the academic and holistic standards for college admissions. The goal of the UC prompts is not to display the student's writing abilities or skills, although they are imperative to the process, it is of greater importance to emphasize compelling content.

**Q: How important is the essay? In your experience, has it ever made the difference between a student being accepted or not?**

**A:** The essay is essential to the admission process if used appropriately. It has been my experience that the personal statement can offer valid explanation for transcript trends or highlight a general activity or experience from a unique perspective. If there are any discrepancies in the student's application, the reader will often look for an explanation in the essay portion of the application.

**Q: Is there anything that a student might find surprising either about your selection process or about what you are looking for in the essays?**

**A:** Authenticity and ownership are two of the most important elements of a personal statement. Be honest, take responsibility for any mistakes or missteps and illustrate growth and development. Some parents and students are surprised to discover that the selection process will acknowledge students for marked academic improvement. It is important to own any mistakes if they visibility affected the student's academic performance.

> Jasmine Thompson has more than 10 years' experience working in the nonprofit, public and private sectors. She holds her bachelor's degrees in Psychology and African American Studies from the University of California, Davis (2006) and recently completed her master's degree in Counseling from St. Mary's College of California where she completed her thesis on The Adaptive Role of Black Fathers and African American Families (2011).

**KIM GLENCHUR**
**Former Reader, University of California freshman applications**
**Educational Consultant, CollegesGPS**

**Q: Can you give students an idea of what happens to their applications and essays after they are received by the college?**

**A:** UC details "How applications are reviewed" on its website. There is nothing magic about this process, though applications are now in electronic form instead of on paper. The last day to submit a freshman UC application is November 30th. Applications are distributed to selected campuses. High school GPAs are recalculated for the 10th and 11th grades, and test scores are linked to applications. In the latter half of December, application reading begins as do any follow-up inquiries to students. Human beings read each application one-by-one, despite the daunting numbers of freshman applicants applying for the Class of 2017:

| | |
|---|---|
| UCLA | 80,472 |
| UC Berkeley | 67,658 |
| UC San Diego | 67,403 |
| UC Santa Barbara | 62,402 |
| UC Irvine | 60,619 |
| UC Davis | 55,877 |
| UC Santa Cruz | 38,507 |
| UC Riverside | 33,809 |
| UC Merced | 14,966 |

[Figures from Table 1 at http://www.ucop.edu/news/factsheets/2013/13app.html]

The priority deadline for financial aid is March 2, and admission decisions with financial aid packages are sent to students later that same month.

The UC Regents Policy on Undergraduate Admissions and California Proposition 209 provides the basis for student eligibility. Each UC campus establishes its own procedures for determining admission because of differences among the applicant pools. At UC Berkeley, every application is read at least twice and by different readers. Every reader is trained not only before the reading process begins, but also during the reading process to assure standardization of evaluations. Readers must avoid conflicts of interest and recuse themselves from reading the applications of acquaintances.

**Q: What specific advice do you have for the freshman applicant prompt?**

*Describe the world you come from—for example, your family, community or school—and tell us how your world has shaped your dreams and aspirations.*

**A:** For this first prompt, the critical information is a student's context of opportunities, not a family history. Know that your application will be evaluated within the context of your environment. Families and schools vary in the resources available to them. Did you take advantage of academic and extracurricular opportunities? What were they and what were the outcomes? If you decided that such opportunities were not for you, and you have no plans for participating in the life of a residential college campus, you might want a degree from a commuter or online college instead.

Many students lament that they have not had to overcome adversity and thus write an essay about the life of a forebear, usually a grandparent, who made good despite all. This tells the reader nothing about the student. For students who have not had to overcome hardships, a good read is Bill Gates' 2007 Harvard commencement address in which he states, "From those to whom much is given, much is expected." *Carpe diem* is Latin for "seize the day." Avoid passivity and shape your own world.

The second part of the prompt hints at how you have come to this point of applying to college. Think hard about the purpose of your *undergraduate* application—e.g., you are not applying to medical or law school though you may have given it some thought. Why do you want to go to *college* and a UC at that? Be aware of what you are writing. On one hand, many majors such as nursing, business or aerospace engineering are not found at all UC campuses, so it would be odd to aspire to an area not academically supported at the UC campus to which you're applying. On the other hand, if you have no prospective major in mind, decide whether the campus could be a place where you could thrive.

**Q:** **What specific advice do you have for the second prompt for all applicants?**

*Tell us about a personal quality, talent, accomplishment, contribution or experience that is important to you. What about this quality or accomplishment makes you proud and how does it relate to the person you are?*

**A:** Ask yourself: What makes you special or what do you like to tell people that you've done? The second part of this prompt asks for your take on the impact or effect that this quality or accomplishment has had on you. This essay could be a great opportunity to discuss your next step of continued development at UC.

**Q:** **What are some of the most common mistakes that students make when writing their essays?**

**A:** The biggest mistake is when applicants don't answer the prompts to talk about themselves as people beyond the grades, test scores and activities. Some students waste valuable real estate on the application by repeating their resume or repeating what they've already written. Egregious mistakes are rare but can occur by not thoroughly proofing the essay, such as naming a non-UC institution as being most desirable. The end of an essay can be cut off if the student does not check the maximum word limit. Grammatical errors are distractions.

**Q:** **Are there any topics or approaches to topics that students shouldn't write about?**

**A:** An Internet browser can quickly identify "essay topics to avoid" though exceptions exist depending on how the writing is handled by the student.

To these lists of topics to avoid, I would add: 1) what students think they should study in college to get a good job or please their parents, and 2) California Proposition 209, perhaps unfamiliar to out-of-state students.

It's hard to learn when either your heart is not into the subject matter or you have hell to pay at home for not getting an A. High school transcripts, including those with all A's in non-challenging courses—that is, when challenging ones are available—may be reflecting a reluctance to develop to the next level instead of a real interest in academics. Motivation is everything. While high school is hard, college will be even harder. College-level academics means being able to think on your feet, appraise situations with no obvious right answers, being open to new fields of learning, networking and recognizing opportunities to realize a dream. Life is a journey of personal growth, and the only certainty is change. For some thoughts on motivation and learning, Carol Dweck's *Mindset* provides a good place to begin.

California Proposition 209 states: "The state shall not discriminate against, or grant preferential treatment to, any individual or group on the basis of race, sex, color, ethnicity or national origin in the operation of public employment, public education, or public contracting." Thus, while an essay about race, sex, color, ethnicity or national origin can provide context, they are not factors for UC admission.

**Q: How important is the essay? In your experience, has it ever made the difference between a student being accepted or not?**

**A:** The essay can be very important in providing the context of the student's academic experiences, and thus, can make a difference in the admission decision.

**Q: Is there anything that a student might find surprising either about your selection process or about what you are looking for in the essays?**

**A:** Holistic admissions reviews all parts of a student's application—grades, curriculum rigor, test scores and how one made the most of available resources. Thus, it is possible for a student from a top school with top grades and test scores but little community involvement to be rejected, whereas an A-student with family income responsibilities and scant resources—to gain admission.

> Kim Glenchur is an educational consultant at CollegesGPS (www.collegesgps.com) and a member of HECA, IECA and WACAC. CollegesGPS helps students identify their interests and academic programs to sustain them—which eases the college search, application, essay writing and transition processes.

# 3

# ACADEMIC PASSION

## "J. Paul Getty Museum"

**Sumaya Quillian**
*Accepted by UCLA and UC Santa Barbara*

I WAS RAISED AT THE J. Paul Getty Museum, or at least I felt like I was and I loved it. My dad worked there for ten years from the time I was two years old, and some of my earliest memories are in that museum. When I was in elementary school, my parents and I went there almost every weekend so my dad could get more work done. I loved everything about the Getty, travertine buildings and all. The offices had huge windows overlooking the mountains that let in brilliant sunlight. My mom and I would play hide-and-seek outside my dad's office, and we would run through the dozens of cubicles that formed a maze. With special permission, I was allowed to eat a sugar cube or two from the kitchen. More often than not, I would sneak a few extra ones when my parents were not looking.

Then there was the art. My mom and I spent most of our afternoons at the Getty looking at the collections. I had to see all my favorites each time, the portrait of Maria Frederike, the eighteenth century

French canopy bed, and the oil painting of Princess Leonilla. Even now, I remember most of the exhibitions that I saw; everything from the sculptures of Jean-Antoine Houdon to the watercolor paintings of Paul Cézanne. Walking through the Central Garden was my favorite way to end the day. There were some days in the spring when the sky was a vivid shade of blue, every plant was in full bloom, and being in that garden felt magical. Few kids can say that they have their own museum, but the Getty is mine, and no one can tell me differently.

When my dad left the Getty to take a new job, I thought I was going to lose a part of myself after ten years. Until high school, I did not realize that I could never lose my museum, and I could never lose the passion that I gained for the arts. After all the times I spent at the Getty, I saw the incredible works that people can create. I was able to see the heights of creativity and intellect come alive, and the art inspired those things in me. Even though I am not an artist, I hope to be always immersed in the arts; visiting renowned museums around the world, hearing symphonies perform in concerts, and seeing dramatic works on the stage.

## ANALYSIS

Not many of us got to grow up playing in the Getty Museum, and in some ways it might seem like Sumaya has an incredible advantage in this experience alone. But the way in which Sumaya discusses her experience emphasizes her childhood curiosity and joy, rather than privileged access to art and culture, and she is able to take away an understanding of her relationship to art that extends to all areas of her life—the essay is much more about Sumaya's childhood curiosity and her ongoing appreciation for art wherever she can find it, rather than special access to the Getty.

Sumaya wonderfully recaptures the sense of the joys of childhood, mundane and spectacular alike. She begins, for instance, her account of her weekends spent at the Getty with her father by focusing on, of all things, his office—the huge windows, the view, the cubicles and the sugar cubes. She lavishes description on these things, and the reader understands just what an exciting place even this office was to young Sumaya: "The offices had huge windows overlooking the mountains that baked in the brilliant afternoon sun. My mom and I played hide-and-seek in the maze of cubicles outside my dad's office."

The fact that there is a museum attached to the office becomes almost an afterthought: "Then there was the art." The way in which

Sumaya specifies her favorite pieces and recounts how "I had to see all my favorites each time" really captures the experience through a child's perspective—the childlike listing of her favorites and the almost petulant insistence that she see them even mimics a child in tone.

For Sumaya the Getty as a whole is an experience—the office, the view, the gardens, as well as the art. We understand the importance of art to her not only as something she appreciates viewing, but as a part of a greater experience of childhood curiosity and connection to her family.

Most importantly, Sumaya takes this experience and applies it to her broader life in a very organic way: we understand from the first two paragraphs of the essay just how integral the experience of the Getty, specifically, is to Sumaya's life, and when her father takes a new job, we can understand her bewilderment and sense of loss—until she recognizes that her experiences at the Getty have left her with an appreciation for art and creativity that is in no way limited to that museum alone. In making the reader see vividly exactly how important every aspect of the Getty was to Sumaya, in lavishing detail on even the most mundane of memories, we understand that the Getty and its art was truly a part of Sumaya, and how she still carries with her the same appreciation even after her link to the Getty is severed.

## "Ocean Institute"

**Hayley Ritterhern**
*Accepted by UCLA and UCSD*

*Essay prompt: Personal quality, talent, accomplishment, contribution or experience*

IN 6TH GRADE, BEFORE ELEMENTARY SCHOOL suffered major budget cuts, my school was asked to appoint students as trainees with the Ocean Institute (OI) in Dana Point, California. My demonstrated interest in science won me the coveted representative spot from my class. At age 11, I stood confidently before a crowd of visitors as a student docent and proudly told them about the gastric pouches on the moon jelly ("they turn pink when they're full of yummy brine shrimp!"). That was not the first time I realized how interesting it is to experience science hands-on, but it was the first time I discovered how much satisfaction I received from sharing that unique knowledge with others. Now I love explaining cool science information that most people don't know, to people that tend to be awed by the things I show them.

At the requisite age of 14, I applied to become a Public Programs docent and have remained committed to OI ever since. My docent experience allowed me to work on the maintenance of the Remote Operated Vehicle (ROV) exhibit under the care of the sea-worn engineer. At first I didn't know the difference between a screw driver and a hammer, but eventually I plunked the renovated ROV in the water and it buzzed around good as new. The kids waiting patiently lit up in smiles as they tried to maneuver the ROV's camera to look at our faux deep sea life in the tank. For the first time, I saw the important connection between engineering and biology, which pushed me to apply for the Rose-Hulman research internship on biomedical engineering.

My docent position allows me the opportunity to continue sharing my excitement about ocean awareness. Whether teaching people about the two-spot octopus, and why there is a Mr. Potato-Head in its tank (enrichment toy for food!), or working alongside researchers in our labs, I love seeing the visitors' looks when they discover crazy little quirks about our ocean life. Their reactions led me to brainstorm ways for more students to visit the institute. I initiated "Operation Environmental Outreach," to fundraise and organize for a class in an underprivileged Hispanic neighborhood to come down to the OI and participate in a science curriculum enrichment program. With the assistance of the chapter of the Science National Honor Society which I established at my high school, I hope to see this project grow each year.

The experience of working at the OI validated my predisposition for science in general, and my philosophy about spreading information about ocean awareness to our community. Whether it was tinkering away on a new ROV to explore ocean life, or witnessing the birth of a baby skate, the Ocean Institute has inspired me to continue pursuing the bridge between engineering and lives of organisms. I cherish my memories of the sea life I observed and the children I have met who inspire me to keep sharing my quirky love of science!

## ANALYSIS

Hayley's essay chronicles the development of a student with true intellectual vitality. Hayley is able to take a passion she discovered in 6th grade and devote herself to it throughout her entire high school career. This commitment to a single academic project is impressive, but Hayley goes beyond being a well-developed scholar. She also commits herself to educating those around her, and thus creating an academic community.

The essay opens with an anecdote about how Hayley got involved in OI in 6th grade. This story gives us background on the type of student Hayley is. Even at a young age, Hayley impressively possesses a "demonstrated interest in science." Furthermore, Hayley demonstrates the extent of her self-proclaimed "interest in science" by describing her first time as a docent in the OI. Hayley talks about the specific knowledge she attained, but the language she uses is not overly technical. Instead, she re-creates the words of an 11 year-old girl, delighted by her work. Hayley's parenthetical about moon jelly pouches ("they turn pink when they're full of yummy brine shrimp!") gives the reader a sense of Hayley's voice and a taste of her genuine love of oceanography.

Hayley continues to do this throughout the essay. She invites the reader into her head, giving us a sense of how she thinks and what facts she finds exciting. These parentheticals are spread evenly throughout the essay so they do not become overwhelming. Instead, they act to constantly remind the reader that Hayley is being sincere with her descriptions.

The essay carefully describes how Hayley used each of her experiences at OI to become more engaged in her academic community. Her work with the ROV inspired her to try biomedical engineering with the Rose-Hulman research internship. Likewise her love of teaching others while being a docent inspired her to start Operation Environmental Outreach. This information gives context as to how Hayley became involved in the activities that are already listed on her application. Furthermore, it suggests that Hayley possesses the initiative to take what she is doing and engage in it in new and dynamic ways. Hayley proves that she enjoys constantly acquiring new skills, cultivating her interests and building upon those interests to seek new challenges.

Still, even when listing her multiple projects, this essay doesn't read like a brag sheet. Instead of simply describing all of her accomplishments and discussing why she became involved, Hayley tells a story. We watch as she moves from one thing to another, constantly being driven by her passion to share knowledge with others. In every single paragraph, Hayley mentions how important it was to her that she was able to inspire kids, excite adults or otherwise engage others in her academic pursuits. These details depict Hayley as a student who is motivated purely by academic enrichment in all of its forms. The result is a well-written essay that successfully illustrates Hayley as a student who thrives in the creation of an engaging academic community.

## "Book"

**Jessica R. Weinman**
*Accepted by UCLA*

*Essay prompt: Personal quality, talent, accomplishment, contribution or experience*

MY EXPERIENCE WITH BOOKS STARTED WHEN I was in elementary school. We were learning, as children do in the primary grades, how to read and write. I had no particular love of reading; I just saw it as something I had to do for school. I went on this way into middle school. One day, my mom wanted to stop at the bookstore for a cookbook. I found myself wandering around the kid's section. This was when I saw the Harry Potter book display. I, like many others, had seen the first Harry Potter movie. I thought it was a good story, but I wasn't really interested in it. This day, I picked up the book, turned the first pages, and landed on the dedication page. It said, "For Jessica, who loves stories."

Of course, I am not the Jessica that the author was speaking of, but imagine my surprise. It was almost as if the book were speaking specifically to me. I went on to read the first chapter, barely hearing my mom when she told me it was time to leave. I had discovered the main difference between the written word and movies; my own imagination. I found that what an individual brings to a story, his or her unique background, makes the same story different for each person. This was when my passion for reading first came to light. Books change me because I continue to think about them long after I have finished reading them; few movies have this lasting effect. Books teach things that aren't always in a curriculum, that really make me think. Science fiction and fantasy can show me cultures and places that may never exist, while nonfiction teaches me about cultures and places that do exist.

This led to my headfirst dive into fiction of all kinds, sparking my passion for reading. My love for words is now a personal quality that I know will never leave me. As I think back to the differences between books and movies, I realized that I also learned to be open-minded from this experience, and now I try not to shut out new ideas. This has extended from books to magazine, newspapers, and articles that can be found all over the internet. Any critical thinking skills I have can be attributed to my time spent online, rummaging through articles to ferret out an interesting, or important, or factually correct article.

This is now seen as a strength of mine by many people I know. Not only do I read quickly and thoroughly, but I also read many genres, such as science fiction, fantasy, and nonfiction of all kinds. When someone is looking for a new book to read, they usually ask for my opinion. I have often been told that my suggestions helped someone to find a new series or genre that they liked. Then, they come back to ask for more advice and share their favorite books in turn, which expands my outlook even more. I feel very proud that my peers respect my literary opinions.

Reading has changed me as a person, from little references I make when I speak, my vocabulary, and trivia to the way I think and look at the world. I know that reading will be a lifelong passion of mine.

## ANALYSIS

This essay about a passion for books stands out from the crowd of essays on the same theme. While Jessica does make some generic statements ("I found that what an individual brings to a story, his or her unique background, makes the same story different for each person;" "My love for words is now a personal quality that I know will never leave me."), she provides meaty evidence to back them up. Her clear writing and use of details gives this essay heft and reveal her personality. These techniques separate her essay from one that deals in generalities about why reading is great and make it ring true.

Jessica begins this essay with a vignette that includes a vivid surprise at the end. The striking coincidence that J.K. Rowling dedicated her book to another Jessica catches the reader's attention just as much as it did young Jessica's. It may have made the essay even stronger to begin with this story, rather than opening with a description of the very beginning of her reading history.

Jessica enlivens her essay by fleshing out exactly what she enjoys about reading. She notes, "Books change me because I continue to think about them long after I have finished reading them; few movies have this lasting effect." In this sentence, she employs a simple and direct writing style to make an insightful observation about her reading experience. This sentence provides much more information than would the statement "Books change me" on its own; Jessica's version adds content to an otherwise pat declaration. She goes on to detail what appeals to her about science fiction and nonfiction, respectively, further elucidating why she reads.

Jessica uses her description of herself as a reader to communicate who she is as a person. She mentions how reading activates her imagination and teaches her to be "open-minded" and fosters her "critical thinking skills." Not only that, but she shows how important reading is to her identity by explaining that her social circle recognizes her expertise: "When someone is looking for a new book to read, they usually ask for my opinion." Her comments about the trading book suggestions and opinions underscores her intellectual curiosity and ability to learn from others. All of these qualities are crucial to success in college, no matter one's field of study.

Jessica's conclusion provides some good details about ways large and small in which reading has affected her: "from little references I make when I speak, my vocabulary, and trivia to the way I think and look at the world." Though this sentence could use some polishing to improve its grammatical structure, it is more effective than her final line because it is more detailed and original. It could stand on its own without the last line as a conclusion to an essay that reveals a student who engages as actively and openly with life as she does with reading.

## "Desires for Knowledge"

**Kris Thompson**
*Accepted by UC Berkeley, UC Davis, UC Irvine and UC San Diego*

JUST LAST WEEK, MY PHYSICS TEACHER introduced the revolutionary (and often times quite complicating) theory in which time is relative to the speed at which one travels.

Up until this point, Special Relativity was only a subject in a Calvin and Hobbes comic strip from years ago. This prompted a discussion with my friends, all of whom were as interested in the subject as I, wherein the common conception of time being the fourth dimension came about. I had to wonder: since we live in a dimension consisting of three spatial dimensions plus the dimension of time, are there more dimensions out there? If one existed in a universe of greater dimensions, it seems possible that time would not play as significant a figure.

Such an experience of timelessness, as it were, would be personally fascinating; for, it always seems as though there is never enough time. As cliché as it may seem, many memories of mine do indeed seem like they occurred yesterday and though I may only be a 17 year-old student, I can still remember first entering high school as a freshman. I can remember the day I got my first dog back in the third grade. Yet, here I am, on the brink of entering a university. It just seems though there is never enough time to truly experience all the wondrous things in life. And so, to even imagine that there may exist a place wherein a continuous feeling of nostalgia is possible, is in my opinion quite exciting.

## ANALYSIS

Questions asking applicants to expound on their own intellectual interests may seem like an opportunity to show off knowledge, but savvy applicants know that there's much more at stake than simply demonstrating how much they know or how deep their knowledge of one particular subject goes. In this short answer essay, Kris economizes on space by leaving the concept of special relativity a fairly nebulous one (which reinforces the reader's sense, as Kris says, of its "complicating" and "fascinating" nature). Rather than trying to explain a complex concept, he focuses both on the way that he and his friends approach novel concepts and new subjects, and on his thought experiments, in which he applies the theory to his own life and experiences.

In mentioning the conversations he has with his friends about special relativity, Kris is able to illustrate a lively intellectual milieu among his friends outside of school, suggesting that his scientific curiosity and academic thinking extend beyond the classroom. The question that the discussion leaves him with ("since we live in a dimension consisting of three spatial dimensions plus the dimension of time, are there more dimensions out there?") and his proposed answer ("If one existed in a universe of greater dimensions, it seems possible that time would not play as significant a figure.") may or may not be a particularly nuanced application of special relativity—which one wouldn't expect or demand from a seventeen-year-old! However, it does demonstrate Kris' curiosity and his desire to seek further knowledge, to hypothesize based on theories and existing knowledge and to examine the hypotheses he formulates.

Kris then leaves the nuts-and-bolts world of physics and his own musings on the possibilities the theory of special relativity entails and he brings it into his own life—he recalls major events in his life, such as getting his first dog and entering high school, emphasizing and thus juxtaposing both his relative distance in time from these events as well as the sentimental proximity he feels for them. Space permitting, Kris could benefit here from some specific and more personal details about these events, particularly since he wants to evoke the nostalgia he feels when he reflects on them, but despite the relative impersonality with which he treats them, he still communicates his ability to expand on academic theories and concepts and examine them in light of their personal significance to him and his own life and experiences. He ends with a slightly fantastical notion, envisioning a timeless world, "wherein a continuous feeling of nostalgia is possible," which leaves the reader with a sense of Kris' strong imagination, backed by pervasive and thoughtful academic curiosity.

## "World"

**Jessica R. Weinman**
*Accepted by UCLA*

*Essay prompt: Describe the world you come from and how your world has shaped you*

MY WORLD IS SIMILAR TO THE world of many others. My world consists mainly of family, home, and school. The great things about my world are the differences that change the word "home" to "*my* home," that make me who I am.

My family from the outside might look like an average family; two parents and a sister. But they are more than that to me. These individuals have influenced me throughout my life. They have all been supportive in everything I do. They have encouraged my loves of reading and computers, from reading to me and with me, to listening patiently as I explain the differences between C and C++. We do community service together at Frontline Foundation and eat dinner together almost every night. I've realized that while my family is typical, I am different.

My family is Jewish. I am not. Most children follow their parents' religion, at least until they are older. As an atheist, this schism has changed my outlook toward others. Realizing that what I believed was different from what my parents, sister, cousins, aunts, uncles and grandparents all believed, but not discussing it for years, made me feel like an outsider of sorts, although none of them ever realized it. When my mom found out, she was surprised but supportive. She understands that every individual has a right to her own beliefs, but was nevertheless disappointed that mine were different from hers.

My school is also quite unique. High Tech Los Angeles is not like any other school I have seen. It is smaller, for one thing, so the teachers connect with the students much more easily than those in a large school. HTLA offers no AP classes and very few Honors classes, which makes our curriculum unique from that of LAUSD schools. My school's philosophy is that not being competitive, and just learning for the joy of it, would spark our inquisitive natures. There are no bells; we have to get to class on time without any help or warnings. Technology is integrated into almost every class, so we learn about computers almost subconsciously. I thought I was on my way to being a lawyer, as I had grown up learning bits of law from my parents, when my high school opened my mind to Computer Science and other technologic fields. My school has changed who I am and who I will be.

My newfound love of technology led me to seek out other programs in the field, and that is how I found COSMOS. I went twice, once to UC Irvine and once to UC San Diego. Both programs changed me in different ways. The first time, I learned about independence in general. Having never been away from home, this was a completely new experience for me. It was nice to learn that I can thrive on my own. The second time, I established my passion for computers. At UC San Diego, I learned how to code using the C programming language. This experience reinforced my passion for computers and influenced my dreams and aspirations for the future, which I know will involve some form of technology.

So, yes, my world might look like any other when seen from the outside. From the inside, however, my world is my own.

## ANALYSIS

The strength of Jessica's essay is its detailed articulation of how she found and pursued a passion for computer science. No reader could mistake her sincere zeal for the subject, nor her consistent effort to develop her knowledge of the field. She could have zeroed in on this central topic sooner in the essay, rather than including short explanations of other parts of her world, such as her family and her religion. Nonetheless, she weaves her interest in computers into this seemingly-unrelated information by describing how her family members "have encouraged my loves of reading and computers, from reading to me and with me, to listening patiently as I explain the differences between C and C++."

The paragraph on Jessica's "unique" high tech high school is the heart of this piece. By describing her high school, she explains its strengths and implicitly describes her own skills. Since Jessica goes to a school that enables students to "learn about computers almost subconsciously," readers can assume that she has developed a nearly-subconscious comfort and aptitude with computers. Jessica's enthusiasm for her school conveys her passion for learning and allows her to describe her own important and unusual abilities without overt bragging. At the same time, she gives admissions officers some crucial information about her school to explain something that might otherwise come across as a weakness of her application: she has taken no AP classes and at most a few honors classes. Jessica makes clear that this is due to lack of opportunity rather than lack of motivation, and suggests that her high school's non-competitive environment has "sparked . . . [her] inquisitive nature." Keep in mind that an open-ended essay question is an excellent chance to provide admissions officers with information and justification that does not fit elsewhere in your application. As in this example, it gives you space to provide your own take, in your own words and with your own "spin," on potential red flags in your application.

Jessica also shows how her interests have changed and grown over time. She describes her decision to pursue computer science, despite her family's legal bent and her own initial inclinations in that direction. Including this detail demonstrates that she has come to a mature decision and has the independence of mind to discover her own interests. She also describes how learning to code at COSMOS strengthened her desire to learn more about computer science. The essay highlights her participation in a selective program and her previous experience in a college environment. Beyond simply namedropping this fact, Jessica gives specific details about how each summer at COSMOS affected her growth.

Jessica's essay not only shows her dedication to computer science, but also provides a detailed window into how she became so dedicated to the subject. Along the way, she paints a vivid picture of how her high school experience and her summer learning set her apart from the average applicant.

### "Academic Preparation"

**Stephanie Anderson**
*Accepted by UCLA and UC Santa Barbara as a transfer student*

SINCE MY YOUTH, READING HAS BEEN my greatest passion and joy in life. My mother learned by the time I was eight years old not to buy me books, knowing I would finish them within hours of getting home from the store. I instead took out scores of books from the library at a time. In middle school, I read at least a book a day and even now, my friends know the surest way to my heart is to recommend a new author.

Clearly books are my passion, however since entering college I have studied business and accounting, viewing accounting as a career that would give me reasonable assurance of financial security. It is only recently that I have acknowledged that this path will not assure personal fulfillment. A month ago I finally spoke with a counselor about changing my major to English in order to pursue a career in publishing. I have little practical knowledge in the field, however my unsatisfying experience in other fields of work and my life-long passion for reading have strengthened my resolve to pursue publishing. I am confident that I will find fulfillment in the literary field, and that satisfaction is worth more to me than any salary could provide.

## ANALYSIS

This essay serves a very utilitarian purpose in Stephanie's application: to explain why she has changed her academic goals and pursuits although already on the business and accounting path in college. But rather than seeming like a justification or a defense, Stephanie presents her situation in a very touching and personal way, and secures the reader's sympathy while also offering a brief (necessarily, given the short answer length) glimpse into what makes Stephanie tick as a person.

Stephanie begins with her childhood and her ongoing passion for reading, beginning by telling the reader what she is passionate about, rather than starting out with a justification or explanation. Instead, she offers us a brief and personal view of the joy she took in reading as a child and the joy she continues to find in it. The personal detail, for instance, that her mother had to stop buying books for her and instead get them from the library, or that her friends often recommend new authors to her, also shows us something of Stephanie's family life and her social relationships and the centrality of reading to them. Stephanie might benefit from some more specific details—which new authors, for instance, or which books stand out vividly from childhood?—but overall manages in a few short sentences to convey to us the ongoing pleasure that reading continues to provide to Stephanie in her life.

She contrasts that in her next paragraph with business and accounting, and her considerably less joyful utilitarian observation that "accounting as a career . . . would give me reasonable assurance of financial security." The difference between the flowing and effusive tone with which Stephanie discusses reading and the rather flat and joyless assessment of accounting is fully palpable, and it is with this artful contrast that Stephanie communicates how important, how necessary it was that she choose to pursue her passion rather than a comfortable but thankless salary.

In her third paragraph, Stephanie is frank about her lack of background and experience in her new chosen field, publishing, but the rapport that she has established and the sympathy she has garnered with her readers with her honesty in her first two paragraphs makes her frankness about her inexperience refreshing. Stephanie has already won the reader's confidence by so forcefully and skillfully communicating the contrast between her passion for reading and the lack of fulfillment she finds in accounting that it is no stretch for the reader to feel the same confidence when Stephanie says, "I will find fulfillment in the literary field, and that satisfaction is worth more to me than any salary could provide." Stephanie manages to take what can be viewed as a potential weakness and transforms it, with her noticeable shifts in tones and the personal detail she injects into her stories about reading as a child, into a reason to root for her.

# 4

# BOOKS/LITERATURE

## "The Champion of the World"

**Ben L.**
*Accepted by UCLA and UC Davis*

I DON'T LIKE ENGLISH. I DON'T mean the language; I love speaking English. I mean the class. Since the moment we began to analyze *The Phantom Tollbooth* in sixth grade, I have never been partial to the subjective examination of literature. I have always been a linear kind of guy; I memorize a sequence of dates in history, I solve for x in algebra. But I never uncover profound meaning within novels—and I thought I never could.

There was a time when I loved to read. Every night and every morning I grabbed my book off the nightstand and immersed myself in adventure. My mom started reading me stories, and I gradually learned to read them myself: *Charlie and the Chocolate Factory, James and the Giant Peach, Danny the Champion of the World*. When I read for pleasure, I read as much as I wanted, for as long as I wanted, and as fast as I wanted. I was absorbed in and concerned with only the exciting and interesting plot.

That changed. School changed, and homework changed. I went from "read a book for half an hour" to "read *The Phantom Tollbooth* chapters 6-9, note especially the universal conflict presented on pages 168-173." My reading began to be enforced; my enjoyment and freedom were inhibited. I wanted to read my own book at my own pace. I missed *Danny the Champion of the World.*

I suppose the primary reason for my dislike of English was my inability to understand it and do well in the class. We read a book, we talked about symbols and motifs and themes and imagery and parallels. I was intimidated! How was I supposed to know that stars represented destiny? I just kept searching for the systematic approach to analysis, the formula to determine symbolism. Why couldn't we just choose a book to read and write a summary of it? Hey, it worked in elementary school.

It is only now that I am beginning to understand that my struggle has been worthwhile. I have come to realize that the skills I have learned as I analyze literature have helped me to think analytically in other areas of my life. I no longer accept political ideas and proposals; I question their purpose. I no longer see a piece of art, admire it, and move on; I probe the thoughts of the artist to determine what he is trying to express. And even though I still dislike analyzing literature, I finally recognize that it teaches me to think critically, to explore myself, and to push my limits.

I always wanted to go back to *Danny the Champion of the World;* I was too scared to push myself and wanted to hide within my comfort zone. Forget Danny. I am the champion of the world now. English class has taught me to think for myself and to take risks, and I will use these skills for the rest of my life.

## ANALYSIS

At first glance this essay seems a bit like Ben as he presents himself in the beginning of his essay: simple, straightforward, and likeable. Ben makes simple declarative statements; he announces what he is like and takes it for the gospel truth ("I don't like English . . . I solve for x in algebra"); he presents a conversational, confessional tone with plenty of goofy humor ("I don't mean the language . . . I mean the class").

But the point of this essay is that the experience of institutionalized literary analysis as he encountered in high school, while ultimately not Ben's cup of tea, made it apparent to Ben that he was more than a simple, straightforward, "solve for x" kind of guy. Likewise, it becomes apparent that this essay is more than a simple, straightforward essay.

To begin with, Ben presents a really artful contrast between his persona as he presents it at the beginning of the essay versus how he appears at the end. He begins with concrete declarative statements at the beginning; simple, direct, to the point, even getting into a clipped and efficient cadence. His resistance to literary analysis as he is introduced to it with the *Phantom Tollbooth* is similarly presented in short punctuated sentences—practically mimicking a petulant child and reinforcing the sense that Ben gives at the beginning of the essay that he is linear and set in his ways.

But in the fifth paragraph Ben's cadence changes: he becomes introspective; his sentences become longer, and he even adopts an artistic pattern of repeated sentence beginnings ("I no longer accept political ideas and proposals; I question their purpose. I no longer see a piece of art, admire it, and move on; I probe the thoughts of the artist to determine what he is trying to express."). The stylistic flourishes that Ben puts on this paragraph in the end of his essay completely undermine the sense that Ben is not a "literary" kind of guy, which is precisely what is happening in the narrative in Ben's essay.

But Ben's stylistic touches don't go too far: they are completely congruent with the conversational, personal tone of his essay and we take "Forget Danny. I am the champion of the world now," not as self-aggrandizing or pompous, but as a tongue-in-cheek and nicely-turned phrase. Ben's reminiscences on his childhood, too, and his frank admissions of feeling challenged and disliking what challenges him render him even more likeable, and we can sympathize with the shock of having to analyze books rather than simply read them. The fact that Ben encapsulates what was actually a very long process of coming to terms with literary analysis and realizing its greater application to other areas of his life and scholarship in a single episode organized around having to switch out reading *Danny the Champion of the World* for analyzing *The Phantom Tollbooth* helps keep him focused, and the anecdote format lets Ben give nice touches of personal detail, leaving the reader with the sense that he has genuinely gotten to know Ben.

# 5

# CAREER

## "Breaking Free of the Chains of a Corner Office"

**Cristina H. Mezgravis**
*Accepted by UC Irvine and UC Riverside*

*Essay prompt: Personal quality, talent, accomplishment, contribution or experience*

"WHAT IS YOUR GOAL IN LIFE?" he asked. I stared blankly at the computer screen, at the young man who stared back at me, patiently waiting for an answer. I pictured myself walking around a picturesque campus, my arms wrapped around books, busily headed somewhere. "Well, I want to graduate from a good college . . . ," I started to say self-consciously.

"No," my friend interrupted, "What is something huge you would fight to death for?" As I bit my lower lip and looked down at the keyboard, I could feel him starting to smile. I furrowed my brow in confusion, in realization, and just as I started to resent him for mocking my seemingly pointless life, he continued, "Do you want to win a Nobel Prize? Be remembered as one of the greatest poets of all times? What do *you* want, deep down, your obituary to say?" I was struck by the immensity of what he was suggesting; he wanted me to dream big, to break free of the social conventions by which I bound myself. I remained quiet in thought, as I have a habit of doing, and stared into my past in search of the force that would drive my life.

I used to think this was the same as the question what is your major. I answered that question hesitantly, "Well . . . I . . . like to write, but I want to run my own business, maybe a double-major in business and writing." Then, that day, for the first time, I set these expectations aside, held my breath, gulped, and blurted from my gut, "I want to write a bestseller." I looked up slowly as I felt myself blush, half-expecting him to burst out laughing.

Surprisingly, no muscle in his face even twitched, "Well, that's it then. You're going to write a bestseller," he said as if commenting on the weather, "You'll have countless doors shut in your face, and you'll leave many editor offices in tears, but if you stick it out without letting that put you down, you'll do it." I sighed with relief and smiled thankfully back at him.

Since then, "a major in Creative Writing" has become my answer to the major question, since that is what will lead to my real goal, but the pressure has never waned. Most listeners have nodded in courteous silence, but I have seen the reflection of my miserable future in their eyes. Other less prudent ones have gone as far as blurting out, "You're going to starve to death!" Repeatedly, I came back to him holding a shattered heart and a trampled self-esteem in my hands, but, eventually, I learned to look at those individuals' pity in the eye with my head held high. It makes me proud that I learned to politely ignore concern from he who studied medicine because Dad's a doctor, she who went to law school to please Mom, or he who sits behind a dreaded desk while life flies by—ironic isn't it? Because I am the kind of person that thinks that if I am to live only once, I'll take starving to death with a pen in my hand and a smile of accomplishment on my face over chaining myself to a corner office in order to achieve "success."

## ANALYSIS

Cristina's essay turns the "experience" essay into a "what's your major?" essay. By discussing the experience of how she chose a major, Cristina is able to flawlessly meld the essay prompt into her examination of her own academic (and career) interests.

The dialogue that opens the essay is intriguing and engaging. Pitting her self-conscious aspirations against the incessant questions of an ambitious peer, Cristina illustrates the tension that she had to face when trying to pick a major. On one hand, Cristina considers herself to be leading a "seemingly pointless life." She doesn't feel like she is doing anything special. That admission is a pretty bold move for a college essay, where the point is to talk about your accomplishments and try to stand out from your peers. However, it works because Cristina is trying to prove most popular professions are "seemingly pointless" or dull in comparison to her more unrealistic desire to write professionally. This is illustrated best in the third paragraph. Her line, "Well . . . I . . . like to write, but I want to run my own business, maybe a double-major in business and writing," sounds as insincere to the reader as it does to Cristina. When Cristina realizes that she was considering business because it sounded like a good major, not because it was something she was passionate about, we consider her conviction to become a writer as a mature and well thought out decision instead of a whimsical one.

In the second half of the essay, Cristina expands upon why she is interested in Creative Writing and the realistic concerns that she has about becoming an author. It would have been easy for Cristina to spend the rest of her essay talking about why she likes writing and what she wants to do with her life. Instead, Cristina lays out the various difficulties she is likely to face and comes to terms with them, adding to our sense of her maturity and thoughtfulness. The dialogue about doors being slammed in her face and the likelihood of starving to death help us better understand Cristina's earlier reservations.

And yet, the essay does not become bogged down with the negative tones of hesitancy and reservation. Rather, Cristina moves on to accept the challenges she is likely to face. She reasonably considers the value in pursuing a career that she is passionate about. She is able to recognize that many students her age do not have the direction or courage to go into a field that hasn't already been picked out for them. In contrast, Cristina shows both direction and great courage in her essay, as well as intellectual vitality. Her final line, about her definition of success, proves that Cristina is pursuing writing simply because it is her academic passion. In turn, Cristina proves to us that her life is driven by her need to cultivate her academic passions.

## "True Happiness"

**Armand Nelson Zenarosa Cuevas**
*Accepted by UC Berkeley*

*Essay prompt: Describe the world you come from and how your world has shaped you*

WHILE GOING THROUGH ELEMENTARY AND MIDDLE school, I was often bombarded with the message, "True success is true happiness." Whether I was watching an after school television special or hearing this lecture from my family, I grew tired of this seemingly cliché message. However, by the time I reached high school, I had greatly matured and was more aware of the world around me. I was surprised at how many people were strongly dissatisfied with their lives, especially when it came to their jobs. From that moment on, I truly appreciated the idea of finding what real happiness is. I realized that expressing my thoughts, feelings, and ideas creatively and openly made me happy. Through this, I could fulfill my dreams of becoming a film director.

After watching television for hours every day at a young age, one could say I was wasting my childhood years. Contrary to the idea that television rots the mind, I am quite grateful for my early exposure to the entertainment medium since it began to strongly pique my interests. As early as seven, I developed original episodes of my favorite television shows in my mind. I would walk around my living room for an hour, creating new episodes of Digimon in my head. At that time, I was extremely embarrassed; to me, it seemed like an odd thing to do. However, this odd thing actually made me happy. In my head, I would create original characters or stories based on existing episodes. I enjoyed making an Excel Document of my own made-up Pokemon, creating my own Pokemon cards, and forming my own music videos inside my head. With my imagination at my disposal, my life was pure bliss.

Entering high school, my fascination with film developed more intensely. By 10th grade, I fully realized my desire to be a film director. I immediately joined the film class at my high school and took advantage of every video project to create movies that my peers would enjoy. I worked meticulously on such projects like my video adaptation of the book, *Catcher in the Rye*, and a film noir involving conspiracies within a high school. I was involved in every aspect of the video production, from directing actors on delivering their lines to finding the perfect music to play during certain scenes; I took great pleasure and pride in every part of my film-making. It was not just film that interested me though, but anything that involved creativity attracted me too. Whether it was writing an article for the school yearbook or thinking of a rap song involving *Lord of the Flies*, using my imagination and inventiveness made me feel truly alive.

Strong support from a loving family coupled with a passionate desire to express my imagination helped me realize that I can make a difference in the entertainment industry. With the industry losing money at the box office and suffering from writers' strikes, I want to bring back the golden age of Hollywood with movies that were both popular and critically acclaimed. With my zest for film and artistic vision at hand, making a name for myself in Hollywood is not far from reach.

## ANALYSIS

Armand discusses two sides of the world he comes from. Both sides have inspired Armand, and helped shape his future aspirations. The first facet is discussed in the opening paragraph of the essay. Beginning with a quote, Armand explains how he grew up that only success is equal to happiness. The people in his life explained how success and happiness were linked, constantly telling him what to aspire to. Meanwhile, Armand saw for himself that this statement was not true. Armand shows extensive maturity in his ability to go against the word of his friends and family and develop his own definition of happiness. In one concise sentence, Armand defines happiness as the ability to express "thoughts, feelings, and ideas creatively and openly." In this way, Armand verbalizes not only what he learned from the world around him, but also how that world shaped his view on the rest of his life.

The rest of Armand's life was shaped by the other world he comes from. This was the world of television. Just like the world of Armand's friends and family taught him how to define happiness, television helped Armand to find it. Although most teenagers grow up watching television, Armand describes his childhood in a way that differentiates his experiences. We see Armand truly immerse himself in the experience of watching television. When he is wandering around his room creating new *Digimon* episodes or making his own *Pokemon* cards, Armand is taking the passive act of watching television and turning it into an active creative process. In this way, Armand proves that he was resourceful, creative and proactive from a young age.

Furthermore, Armand continues his interest in film during his high school career. This dedication reveals Armand's character. As soon as additional resources became available to him in his high school (mainly, a film class), he used these resources to cultivate his passions and refine his art. Armand gives a series of examples of the projects he worked on, giving the reader a sense of the diversity of his skill set. He becomes involved in creating adaptions, finding music, giving lines and directing. Armand's willingness to be involved in filmmaking in several different capacities illustrates his clear passion for his art. Furthermore, Armand is able to intertwine his artistic passion with his academic knowledge. Both the film adaptation of *Catcher in the Rye* and the rap song about *Lord of the Flies* exhibit Armand's ability to interpret literature through art. These projects demonstrate both creativity and artistic maturity.

The final paragraph ties the essay together. Armand turns from discussing the world he comes from and instead recognizing the rest of the world. He acknowledges the issues affecting Hollywood, and provides insights as to what he can do to make a difference. In this manner, Armand suggests how the unique skills and passions he developed during his own life can be used to improve the lives of others.

# 6

# CHALLENGES

## "The Best Presents Sometimes Have the Worst Wrapping"

**Catherine Bronzo**
*Accepted by UCLA*

*Essay prompt: Personal quality, talent, accomplishment, contribution or experience*

"MOTADSÉ!" EXCLAIMED MY GRANDMOTHER IN HER native French. Her sudden shriek was due to her biting into a sour cranberry that I told her was a sweet blueberry. Because of my grandparents' on-setting Alzheimer's disease, I always did the best I could to keep our interactions light and fun, despite the looming grief and loss that inevitably lay ahead. Although I could laugh with them in the moment, it was hard for me to see them deteriorate, never knowing when our last moments together would be.

There were so many reasons why I didn't like what was happening: the potential loss of two people very special to me, as well as an unexpected lifestyle that didn't ask my opinion before barging in. My days for the last three years have not consisted of what I imagined this time period of my life would be like: spending weekends with friends, playing sports after school, going to the movies, or in general just being a "normal teenager." Instead, I was fetching meals, repeating conversations, and providing entertainment to the very same people who used to do the same for me. I constantly told friends that I wouldn't be able to spend time with them on the weekends. My Facebook status and text messages reflected the same sentiment. During my freshman year, I even opted for alternative online schooling for the year, just so I could schedule academics around what was the priority of that time, being a caretaker to my grandparents.

Despite my best attempts to always put on a happy face, my emotions about the situation were mixed and raw. Some of the more intense days required me to make 911 calls, or a trip (or two) to the emergency room. Simpler days may have been spent laughing, holding their hands, or wiping their tears as the confusion took a psychological toll on them.

After three years of watching my grandparents slowly deteriorate, they both finally passed on. My grandfather went first at the end of June 2009 and my grandmother followed half a year later in January 2010. I was devastated. Words could not describe the uproar of feelings conjured up inside me. And I felt it, I felt all of it, staying with the emotion until the very end. But what resounded most inside of me in the aftermath of their death was not sadness, but a question: Now what? For over three years I endured the emotional ups and downs of watching two people I deeply cared for walk the slow road to death. Who was I without this identity?

It took some reflection, but I realized that who I wanted to be was the person I already was. I had initially thought that I may have missed the formative experiences of high school that I needed in order to blossom into the woman I intended to become. But when I looked to see what I missed out on, I knew in my heart nothing could compare to the deep connection I shared with my grandparents before they passed on, not to mention all the responsibility, leadership, and emotional maturity I had learned along the way. I was exactly where I needed to be. I discovered that I wanted to do in life what I had done in a small way for my grandparents— dedicating myself to serving others.

With a small shift in perspective, what I initially thought was an emotionally difficult time period, which resulted in me missing out on precious personal life moments, became my grandparents' gift to me. A great gift, difficult to open and wrapped in emotional turmoil, but the best gift nonetheless: a clear passion and purpose for my life.

I will never forget my grandparents, and this essay is written in memory of them.

## ANALYSIS

Catherine begins her essay with a surprising incident. Her first two sentences, which reveal that she fed her French-speaking grandmother a sour cranberry, leave readers wondering why she would do such a thing. After all, isn't a college essay supposed to show the good side of its author, rather than her trickster side? Once she has captured our attention, she quickly reveals why she pulled this prank and subtly conveys her close, playful relationship with her ailing grandparents. The trick itself is a good metaphor for the whole essay. Catherine manages to avoid an overly sweet tone by tempering her story with more complex flavors. Rather than writing about a personal challenge to plead for pity or to paint herself as a martyr, she uses vivid details to demonstrate her emotional maturity and capacity for self-reflection.

In her second paragraph, Catherine demonstrates the power of following a tried-and-true maxim of good writing: "Show, don't tell." Her two sentences contrasting the life of a typical student with the life of a caregiver use specific, poignant examples ("spending weekends with friends, playing sports after school, going to the movies, or in general just being a 'normal teenager'" vs. "fetching meals, repeating conversations, and providing entertainment to the very same people who used to do the same for me"). The parallel structure of the sentences, which each make use of lists, sharpens the contrast. She also subtly hints at her gratitude and sense of perspective in the phrase "providing entertainment to the very same people who used to do the same for me." Far from depicting herself as a martyr, Catherine matter-of-factly lets the reader know that she is aware of what she herself owes her grandparents. She also slips in information explaining why she spent a year of her high school education taking online courses in a way that does not disrupt the flow of the essay. This is a great example of using an essay as a unique opportunity to explain an anomaly in your transcript to admissions officers.

Catherine gives poignant personal details, such as her description of the range of emotions she experienced as a caregiver. Phrases like "holding their hands" and "wiping their tears" conjure specific, relatable images for the reader that bring her experiences to life. When Catherine relates the facts of her grandparents' deaths, she describes this sad chapter in her life with a distinct purpose and not just to in-spire sympathy. Her rhetorical questions ("Now what?" and "Who was I without this identity?") put the reader in her shoes as she confronts some difficult questions. Although Catherine's final paragraphs some-times err on the side of "telling" rather than "showing," she does clearly state how her time as a caretaker helped her articulate her identity and find a direction for her future. Her closing description of her chang-ing thought processes demonstrates her ability to see multiple sides of an issue and her upbeat—but not naive—reaction in the face of difficulties.

## "My UC Journey"

**Yia Vang**
*Accepted by UC Berkeley and UC Davis and attended UC Davis*

*Essay prompt: Is there anything you would like us to know about you or your academic record?*

COMING FROM A TRADITIONAL HMONG FAMILY, school was a challenge for me even from day one when I stepped off that airplane. The language barrier has always restricted my educational experience and potential: English is not my tongue, and an office not my house. As a bilingual person I realized early on that I must try twice as hard just to be where my peers are at. To understand success and failure I remind myself that we are all humans and can achieve our dreams when there is perseverance to withstand the struggle. Outside of school I have always felt alone on taking care of my schoolwork load because my family is from another country, and I cannot possibly expect them to be experts in education. Taking into account my family's background, I feel lim-ited in expressing my full abilities in school. However, I overcame this disadvantage by pushing myself to take the most challenging classes at each grade level. I have gotten myself many academic opportunities be-cause I saw to it that none should pass me by. During my freshman year in high school I strayed from all my friends by taking Biology Honors instead of a science class with them. The reason for my decision was that the class fitted into the four-year schedule that I had planned for myself as a freshman. In addition, I took Spanish as my foreign lan-guage requirement because living in California I could clearly see how the language will benefit me. As a non-Spanish (sic) and a senior I had doubts about continuing and taking AP Spanish; I do not speak the language outside of school. After being in that class for the first quarter I began to truly appreciate the Spanish language in that I now understand most of what seemed impossible to comprehend three years ago. I have pride in myself for knowing three different languages. I am the first generation of my family's war-torn departure from Thailand, and I want to replace the scythe with the pencil now that I am in America. My parents may not be able to change the quality of life that they and I currently have, but I can. I have no excuse good enough to hide my face if I were to end up feeding on the welfare system; entering America at five years old I had just as fair a shot at my life as any child. Due to family background I am not surprised that very few of my relatives make it to college even if not a UC campus. As my way of aiming higher to get the most I can out of my education, I devote myself to become the first one in my family to attend a UC school. Being brought up in a family where I was not exposed to higher education, I want to personally say that I would have had little or no knowledge of the University of California unless I made the effort to go beyond what I was taught. Because my sister made it to a CSU school, CSU became the goal, the standard, that my parents came to understand. To me strength is the ability to accept that everyone faces challenges in life and that success is sweetest after sweat. My family fled to this country so that I can get an education and not live the lifestyle that they lived; I will repay them and build upon my future by getting a valuable education from the University of California.

## ANALYSIS

This essay topic gives students a chance to describe something important about themselves that cannot be found anywhere else in their application. Note that because of the nature of this essay, it is not as formal as other application essays. The focus is more on the content, rather that the writing itself.

For these reasons, it is no surprise that Yia's prose is a little unconventional; he writes all of his thoughts in one large block, instead of making formal paragraphs. With Yia's writing ability, it may have been hard for him to force what he needed to say into the strict format of one of the first two UC essay topics. However, this final topic allows Yia to focus on just telling his story. Even without the help of good formatting, he gives the audience a clear idea of why he decided to apply to the UC system, the challenges he faced by creating this goal and the importance of the decisions he made along the way.

Although the essay is non-traditional, it still tells a story. We start by hearing about Yia's cultural background. This explains why his English is a bit rough. However, Yia overcomes this language barrier in a way that makes up for his imperfect prose. The essay notes that he strove to improve in English and all academic subjects by taking the most difficult classes offered to him. Of course, Yia's transcript and school report would have shown that Yia took the most difficult classes at his school in each grade. However, the context of this choice is what makes it significant. Yia points out that he went against his friends by taking Honors Biology. He did not have examples to follow from his friends or family, but he did what he could in order to plan for his own future. This decision shows immense foresight and maturity.

As Yia seamlessly continues his narrative, he explains his motivations for taking another difficult course, Spanish. He finds value in the ability to speak Spanish and understands its application to his life, not just his goal of getting into a good college. This is especially clear when Yia discusses the reservations he had about AP Spanish. These reservations are honest and thoughtful. Furthermore, they provide a case study of how Yia deals with hardship in school. He is committed to following through and challenging himself intellectually for his own benefit. These are all qualities of a strong and intrinsically motivated student.

As Yia ends his essay, he notes how all of these academic decisions and family obstacles have cumulated to his goal of attending a UC. This goal now comes off as sentimental to the reader. Despite his reservations about his English language abilities, Yia's passion shows through in his rather poetic writing. The line, "I want to replace the scythe with the pencil" successfully captures Yia's enthusiasm for learning despite his family's difficult history. With this final thought, Yia adds a tone of sincerity to his heartfelt yet informative essay.

## "Who I Am"

**Daniel Hien Vuong**
*Accepted by UC Merced and UC Riverside and attended UC Riverside*

*Essay prompt: Personal quality, talent, accomplishment, contribution or experience*

SOME DAYS WHEN I'M AT HOME I'm a nobody. When I'm up on stage, I'm a somebody.

An inexplicable feeling consumed me as I finished performing. The sound of the crowd reverberated through my mind. I breathed the heavy air of exhilaration. The energy of the crowd surged through me as I finished a satisfying performance. The last chord has been strummed. The last verse has been sung. The roaring of the crowd continues as I walk backstage.

Being a performer and entertaining the audience is my proudest accomplishment. I recall sitting in the crowd at a concert, wanting so badly to be the man on stage, wielding the guitar, singing his heart out. But I told myself that I would never be up there because my shyness would always keep me from doing so. Here I am a couple of years later and I'm the performer. The journey was long and definitely difficult.

It all started with high school. Entering a new environment was a scary thing for me. I was shy and uncomfortable amongst strangers. It would help if I was well-known for something, but I wasn't. To my friends, I was just a patient friend who they'd come to when they needed advice. To others, I was impossible to single out in a crowd. I wasn't the dancer nor the smart guy. I was just your average kid. And as an average kid, my confidence level was not very high.

Although I envied the musician on stage, I did not have any real intentions to become a performer myself. At the same time, I was interested in learning how to play the guitar because I wanted to be known for something amongst my friends. But as my knowledge and skills progressed, so did my confidence.

The first time I was up on stage I was really nervous. I recall anticipating the end of my performance with anxiety. But somehow when I started to play the guitar, everything just clicked. When I finished performing on stage, I felt like the whole world knew my name. I felt like I existed for once. I received cheers and for a couple of days random people complimented me. After a few more performances my popularity shot up. Soon the whole school started to know who I was. I was the guy who could sing and play guitar. I finally accomplished my goal. Performing on stage was no longer a dream, it was reality.

Now I don't want to sound conceited or anything. Don't get me wrong. Learning the guitar and performing on stage gave me popularity, and whilst I do enjoy it a little here and there, popularity was not the only thing that I had gained. Being pressured onto stage and actually performing gave me confidence. No longer do I have to second guess myself when I am in front of people. No longer do I have to worry about anything. I can be myself and still be the performer. I no longer have any doubts, as because I can express myself through performing, I feel that my talent and accomplishment as a performer makes me feel comfortable around people because in the end, they know who I am.

## ANALYSIS

Getting up on stage with a guitar and singing a song might not sound like an earth-shattering accomplishment to some, but for Daniel, those few moments were a pivotal point in his life, one when he marks the change from being a shy "nobody" to becoming a confident, popular performer. Not everyone is an astrophysics genius who found a cure for cancer and painted a masterpiece all before cooking a five-star, four-course breakfast. And even if you are, none of those things might be the talent or accomplishment that is important to *you*.

Not only does Daniel show us how important this "small" moment is to him and why, but he also takes us along with him on his journey from frail freshman to big music man on campus and, in the process, paints a much fuller portrait of him as a person than just a performer.

At first glance the essay might appear a bit average, but Daniel does craft a well-structured composition that both directly addresses the prompt as well as demonstrate an above-average diction ("exhilaration," "reverberated") and balanced writing style employing alliteration ("crowd at the concert," "anticipating . . . with anxiety") and a nice flow of short and long sentences.

Like writing a good sentence, Daniel starts the essay with the most important aspect first: he describes in detail how it feels *to him* during and after a performance. The energy and roar of the crowd. The charge he feels when finished with a song.

After placing us in his shoes, *then* he states his thesis: "Being a performer and entertaining the audience is my proudest accomplishment." And then he immediately *shows* us what he was like before he started performing: the passive, shy spectator. Daniel recognizes and identifies his "faults"—being uncomfortable around strangers, feeling "average"—and gives specific examples that flesh out the "before" picture.

At the same time, Daniel reveals some positive aspects of himself as well: he's patient, he's valued by his friends as a confidant and source of advice, he cares what people think about him and he actively takes charge to improve himself. Average and impossible to single out? Start playing guitar. Shy around strangers? Get up on stage!

And while it would be great to know what kind of songs Daniel performed or what he wants to do with his newfound identity as a musician, Daniel keeps the essay focused on *him* and his journey, and he ends his essay illustrating how the "lessons learned" from his performance experience relate to the development of his character as a whole, a character that, it just so happens, will do very well at a college or university.

## "In the Midst of Every Difficulty Lies Opportunity"

**Carol Nguyen**
*Accepted by UC Berkeley*

LIVING WITH MY MOTHER AND FATHER is not easy. My mother is an immigrant from Vietnam who came here for a better future for her posterity. My father never really respected education—he was born into a rich family in Vietnam, and didn't go to school. Unfortunately, when my father came to the U.S., he lost his money. My mother pushes me to excel academically and pursue a more prominent future, while my father discourages me.

Every day, my mother reminds me that I must rise against all odds. My mother taught me at a young age that education was the key to success. She'd tell me to look around and tell her what I saw. I would declare: a cramped apartment, unsafe neighborhood, and an uninformed community. She'd reply that I had the power to change that. When I work on my English homework late at night, my mother stays up with me, commenting that she doesn't know how to write a simple essay. She reminds me that I am empowered with knowledge and can use it to shape a better future for myself. My mother is my driving force pushing me to reach my potential and steering me in the right direction.

My father has suffered severe health issues. After he was diagnosed with Parkinson's disease he stopped working. From the age of six, I saw my father consume handfuls of pills a day, to cope with his illness, and use an inhaler to treat his asthma. When my mom works weekends, I must care for my father's needs. For the majority of the day, I do my schoolwork until my father calls me to help him. My father has as difficult time doing simple things. When I was young, I would check to see if my father was still breathing right before I went to sleep. Growing up with a sick father is not easy and it's taught me about commitment and discipline. Tending to my father transformed me into a mature, responsible adult.

Comparing my parents is like assessing fire and ice; they're both polar opposites that are volatile when together. My father lived his life without planning his future—and he continues to preach it, although he suffers from heightened health issues. My mother takes care of my father dutifully and reminds me that there's more to life than expecting success will land in my lap. Success must be earned through hard work. My mother's immeasurable efforts to get me to see the possibilities of education have convinced me that determination and resolve will grant me the future that my parents never had.

## ANALYSIS

Carol uses a very matter-of-fact tone to discuss serious and difficult issues she has faced throughout her life. She begins the essay with a to-the-point statement that her parents have been hard to live with, but she avoids sounding at all whiny. Readers can empathize with her predicament and admire her determination because she does not beg for their pity. Instead, she focuses on the encouragement her mom has given her and her commitment to rising above her circumstances. She connects the challenges she has faced to her strong commitment to academics. Rather than portraying herself as a victim, she describes how empowered she feels to create positive change by getting an education. For instance, she brings up her role as a caregiver not to lament the carefree high school life she has missed out on, but rather to note that it taught her "about commitment and discipline" and "transformed [her]...into a mature, responsible adult."

This essay is a good example for any student who is considering writing about personal challenges or tragedies. There are many compelling reasons for using these types of stories in an essay. Difficult life experiences can be defining, in part because the most difficult parts of one's life often inspire the most significant growth and self-reflection. As such, revealing a personal challenge can help admissions officers get to know you better. Providing this kind of information about yourself can also help explain other parts of your application. For instance, maybe you don't have a ton of extracurricular activities to list because you had to devote time to caring for an ill relative or working an after-school job to help support your family. There is little opportunity to convey that information in a college application except in the open-ended format of an essay.

Do not make the mistake, however, of using a personal story like this simply for shock value or because you think it will help you earn sympathy points. A sad experience in and of itself doesn't make you irresistible to college admissions officers. No matter what you've gone through, an experienced admissions officer has read worse. Contrary to myths that might circulate in your high school, a tale of woe isn't an automatic "in." College admissions officers are looking to build the best freshman class they can, not to let in the students for whom they feel the most sympathy. The magic formula is not to make your readers cry, but to demonstrate your ability to learn from trials and to face them with strength of character.

## "Struggling in My Skin"

**Anonymous**
*Accepted by a number of UCs including UC Berkeley, UC Davis, UC Irvine, UC Riverside, UC San Diego and UC Santa Barbara*

*Essay prompt: Personal quality, talent, accomplishment, contribution or experience*

ELEMENTARY AND MIDDLE SCHOOL WERE LITERALLY one of the most painful experiences of my life. It hurt to hold a pencil. It hurt to play with friends at recess. It even hurt to simply sit in class.

I've had a skin condition called eczema ever since I was born. It's chronic, spreads rapidly, flares unexpectedly, and worst of all, there's no cure for it. Eczema caused skin all over my body to turn into raw, burning, and itchy patches. During the day, I constantly fought the urge to scratch myself. At night, I had trouble falling asleep because my skin was on fire. I was convinced that the skin I desperately wanted to step out of would forever inflict torture upon me.

I knew if I really wanted my eczema to go away, I needed to ditch the apathetic attitude I had developed towards my skin. Unnecessary scratching and stress would exacerbate my eczema, but...I guess I couldn't really control these things. And I could always rely on my medicine. However, none of my creams could provide permanent relief.

So, after 15 years of living with my unbearable eczema, I became determined to find a lasting solution. I began to look at my skin in a different way. I was different, and I couldn't live like I had normal skin. Instead, I needed to adopt new habits that suited my eczema.

To address my impulsive scratching, I started filing my nails everyday to keep them short. Before sleeping, I would don a one piece footie pajama, and tie my hands with socks. To relieve my stress, I put my empty planner to use and started to pull less all-nighters. I had always suspected that my eczema was triggered by specific foods, so I started tracking everything I ate. After months of eliminating specific foods from my diet, I discovered that my trigger foods were my favorite foods: dairy and red meat. Instead of reaching for milk in the morning, I went for soy. While my family feasted on cheese pizza, I ate the stale bread from the night before. To my frustration, I didn't see any immediate improvement, but within a few weeks, the burning sensations disappeared. Soon, my weekly flare-ups became rare, and now, I only have the occasional dry crack on my fingers. After months of effort, I had managed to do what none of my medicine had ever done for me.

My eczema has taught me that I need to face my shortcomings and learn how to address them. By accepting my eczema, I found the strength to change a viciously damaging lifetime habit. Now, I can concentrate on my work without squirming from itchiness, and take showers without cringing in pain. For the first time in my life, I feel comfortable in my skin.

## ANALYSIS

One of the best strategies for writing successful application essays is to have the reader walk a mile in your shoes and see the world through your eyes. The writer of "Struggling in My Skin" does just that by slipping you into her skin to *feel* the experience of both having a very uncomfortable condition and, more important, the self-reflection, acceptance and dedication necessary to overcome it.

The writer's success of sharing her story lies within her use of specific sensory diction and concrete details: her skin didn't just hurt, but turned "into raw, burning, and itchy patches" that were "on fire" while she tried to sleep. Her writing style is engaging and easy to read, from the effective use of repetition in the opening paragraph to the skillful combinations of long and short sentences to create a fluid rhythm.

The writer doesn't use her condition to create a "woe is me" plea but instead spends most of the essay sharing *how* her attitude changed and then the specific steps she took to improve herself. The concrete examples she uses to support her story—filing the nails, changing clothes and diet, becoming organized to reduce stress—not only help the reader see who she is as a person, but also shows a maturity and determination that translates into success beyond her skin condition to the challenges of college courses and, indeed, to whatever this woman sets her mind. Universities love to see people be able to self-reflect, take responsibility for their situations and then be able to actively engage in working towards a solution.

Remember that the essay is the best opportunity to present yourself as an individual, and so you should take every chance to include as many aspects of yourself as possible. What other activities and interests were involved when the writer "put my empty planner to use"? And what is her focus now that she's able to "concentrate on my work without squirming from itchiness"? Her engaging and inspiring story makes us want to know more about where she's going and how she's going to apply her lessons learned to her future.

# 7

# COMMUNITY SERVICE

## "Home"

**Anonymous**
*Accepted by UC Berkeley and UC San Diego*

*Essay prompt: Personal quality, talent, accomplishment, contribution or experience*

IF YOU HAD TOLD ME BEFORE I got into the back of a pickup truck headed for Mexico that by the end of the week I would be hanging 22 ft. in the air, upside down, nailing a roof to a house in a city I had never heard of—I would not have believed you. I grew up in a house that always sat quietly in line with all the other houses in my neighborhood, so the mounds of dirt and dust that lined the streets of Mexico, the Mexico I saw, were upsetting. It was a world that I had never visited before, yet once I got there I realized I could never really come back to my house again. A house was something manufactured and common, and suddenly in the cement and sand I saw that a home is something more.

My friend had coaxed me off my comfy summer sofa to join his church group in their annual trip to Mexico, but all I knew how to do was dig. And that is what I did—for ten hours. After about seven hours of shoveling, I couldn't stop. No one could stop, and as the sun fell on the first day and car's headlights illuminated a cement slab and a house's frame—I was proud to be shoveling.

In the middle of the second day, we erected the frame of the house and adults began to devour the jobs that needed to be done. My friend and I were out of work. Ignorant to the difficulty of the task, I suggested we roof the house. I was kidding; I had learned to use a nail gun the day before, I hardly felt capable of roofing a house. But the foreman overheard us, and after we were given permission we climbed the ladder to roof of the first floor. There were three of us up there, and none of us were older than 20.

I have tackled history essays and math tests, but nothing challenged me like that roof in Mexico. I had no textbook for direction, I just learned. Every time my friend corrected a mistake, I got better. Never before had I been so far outside my comfort zone and yet felt so fulfilled. I did not believe I was capable of what I did, and yet I was able to overcome my own limits. Suddenly, I wondered what other worlds lay before me unconquered. If I could roof a house, what else was I capable of?

When the house was finally finished, I took a look around. It no longer looked like a house, or any house I had ever seen before. Beneath the paint, I could see my nails. Poking between sheets of wood, I could see my windows. Hanging from the sky, I could see my roof. The family's tears only transformed the house more; it became a home where a family of strangers had suffered so that a new family would suffer no longer. I never returned to my manufactured world or self inflicted limits. I returned to a home where people struggled, learned, and grew together in something dynamic and evolving—a home. I returned to a world where I could do anything, but more importantly, to a world where I wanted to do everything in order to create homes where there had been houses.

## ANALYSIS

This essay takes on the well-worn subjects of "home" and "service trips." Most admissions officers have tired of these common essay topics. However, although the subject of this essay is a bit hackneyed, the author walks away from this experience with fairly unique insights.

Over the course of his trip, the author learns tangible skills, discovers a passion for learning new things and embodies a willingness to take on challenges. These lessons are what make this essay stand out from others of its kind.

The essay starts out with a captivating image, the young author "hanging 22 ft. in the air, upside down, nailing a roof to a house in a city [he] had never heard of." This description is intriguing, encouraging the reader to find out how the student got into this situation. We then discover that the author had to be "coaxed [ . . . ] off [his] comfy summer sofa to join his [friend's] church group in their annual trip to Mexico." This show of hesitancy doesn't portray the author in the best light. Still, it's honest. Most students don't spontaneously decide to go on a service trip to another country. Giving us his actual motivations—namely, he wanted to be involved in something with his friend over the summer—gives the essay a sense of sincerity.

Having established trust with the reader, the essay goes on to denote important aspects of the author's personal character. The description of the first day of the trip, where the author did nothing but dig, shows that this student is dedicated. Although we know that digging was the only skill the author had going into the trip, when we hear that he was "proud to be shoveling" after 10 hours of work, we know that despite his limited construction skills, he remains humble and driven.

Unsatisfied by the amount he is able to commit to the work of the next day, the author boldly takes on the task of roofing a house with nothing but a nail gun and three other kids under the age of 20. This is bold, and the author's enthusiasm for taking on this daunting task shows great ambition on his part. Despite his lack of knowledge or skill, the author is able to tackle the project, welcoming the challenge with open arms. He works, makes mistakes, gets better and ultimately takes pride in his ability do take on a difficult task in order to learn something new. These skills are ultimately what admissions officers will admire in the author, because these skills will help him continue developing emotionally and intellectually after high school.

The essay then goes back to focus on home and the sense of pride that the author received from making a living space for people less fortunate than him. This conclusion is heartwarming, but falls too much in line with other common service trip essays. The author's lesson about what makes a house a home is not nearly as impactful as what he learned about himself. From this experience the author was able to rid himself of "self-inflicted limits." He learned, he grew and he became excited to try to do more things outside of his comfort zone. It is these lessons that convince us that this student is prepared to take on the many novel challenges of college with fervor.

**"The Next Generation"**

**Nhi Yen Nguyen**
*Accepted by UC Berkeley, UC Davis, UCLA and UC San Diego*

*Essay prompt: Personal quality, talent, accomplishment, contribution or experience*

OVER 110 HOURS OF WORKING, OVER 20 hours of photocopying, and over 5 paper cuts, I managed to complete my Girl Scout Gold Award Project. Establishing an educational enrichment program at a local library, I taught a class of twenty-two students.

Efficient and dedicated, I recruited participants and volunteers and created an authentic learning environment to bolster the children's academic skills in reading, writing, and mathematics. Aimed at giving young students the knowledge and confidence to succeed, my Super Scholars program sported the motto "striving to learn and learning to strive."

Before I began my project, I completed various prerequisites over the course of the year, gaining not only skills in communication and leadership but also in tennis and decoupage. Then, I was ready to embark on my project planning. After researching all possibilities and referencing previous award winners, I took a step back. I separated myself from the orderly construction of the task. I reflected on that which is at the core of all my endeavors: learning. Having grown from all of my experiences, I knew that I wanted to bring this opportunity to others. Since I have been a tutor and teacher's assistant on numerous occasions, I realized that this project would reflect my goals and strengthen my expertise.

In essence, my objective was to establish an impacting program that would empower the young members of the community through education and diverse experiences. Each day, I'd hop out of the car, run over to the library front desk, and patiently wait for the keys to the classroom. Once in the class, I would direct my super team of volunteers and eager pupils to arrange the desks and chairs. Then, proceeding to the white board, I would point out the list of rules with all the students' signatures and ask a student to recite them. Whenever I asked for the program motto, the students would enthusiastically chant the positive words—almost in unison.

We then proceed with the day, going over the core subjects. To enhance the students' learning, I modified the difficulty level of each assignment to each student's particular ability. With encouragement and patience, I tended to each individual's needs. Including interactive games benefitted the learning process. An exciting competition of knowledge definitely kept them focused on the lesson. Nevertheless, the kids would burst into an uproar after the announcement for snack time. After eating some healthy treats, the students had free time to ask the volunteers for additional homework help, draw on the whiteboard, or play a rousing game of pretend.

Ending the day with art, the students delighted in creating tissue paper projects, origami water bombs, etc. The students also enjoyed the activities on theme days focusing on health and water conservation. Exposed to a variety of experiences, the students remained mentally active.

On the last day of class, one of my students ran up and hugged me, thanking me for holding the program. Being naturally social, I enjoyed the opportunity of working with the students and volunteers. Personally, the project was a significant accomplishment. I was able to develop a beneficial project and follow it through with leadership, coordination, and delegation. As a Girl Scout and aspiring activist, I hope to foster a brighter and more confident generation.

## ANALYSIS

Nhi's essay details the service project she completed to obtain her Girl Scout Gold Award. In and of itself, this award is impressive; it is the highest award any Girl Scout can receive (equivalent to the Eagle Scout rank for Boy Scouts). Although Nhi most likely mentioned receiving her Girl Scout Gold Award on her application, the essay provides space for her to elaborate on the importance of this project.

From the beginning, we get a sense of the time and talent Nhi was able to commit to the project. The laundry list of tasks—"110 hours of working, over 20 hours of photocopying, and over 5 paper cuts"— is a quick, neat way to suggest the scope of tasks she had to take on. In addition to her planning the project, we see Nhi teaching, fundraising and recruiting volunteers. The breadth of these tasks shows the diverse scope of Nhi's leadership abilities. More importantly however, this description of how she single-handedly organized her project attests to Nhi's passion for the work she committed herself to.

The reader gains an even greater understanding of Nhi when she describes her motivations for the project. Nhi found inspiration by incorporating something she had to do into something she wanted to be a part of. For example, Nhi had to acquire a multitude of skills including "tennis and decoupage" in order to start her service project. Then, she analyzed what she learned from these seemingly non-related skills and discovered that her own love of learning made each of these experiences memorable. The ability to come to this conclusion shows great introspection, while her realization that not all kids have the opportunity to learn in an engaging environment like she did shows great humility. Together, these details paint the picture of a student who thinks deeply about both others and herself.

After the first half of the essay develops a profile of Nhi as a person, the second half of the essay comments on the impact of her work. An especially moving image of children excitedly chanting the motto and rules illustrates how excited the children in the program are to learn. We see their dynamic classroom incorporates many learning forms including lectures, practice problems, games and art projects. Additionally, Nhi gives details that suggest the breadth of learning going on in her classroom. Snack time is full of healthy snacks and end of day activities touch upon themes such as water conservation. These specifics attest to the amount of thought Nhi put into her work, making it impactful on several different levels.

## "How I Found My Voice"

**Carol Nguyen**
*Accepted by UC Berkeley*

I GREW UP IN A STRICT household that made it difficult for me to find my voice. My parents do not encourage my participation in activities other than academics. I was usually the person in the back who was the keen yet quiet individual, observing from afar, and never had enough courage to speak my mind. During the summer of my junior year I decided to pursue an internship. This decision helped me find my voice.

My father's health condition inspired my decision to find an internship. His Parkinson's disease, asthma, heart issues, and vision problems made me think about my community at large and their access to health information. My curiosity led me to find an internship at the Asian Pacific Health Care Venture in Belmont High School, where I was able to obtain a position as a peer leader. My role was to educate the public about prevailing teenage issues, such as teen pregnancy, nutritional concerns, mental issues, and drug/alcohol abuse. I was trained as an organizer, and felt it was my obligation to inform and aid my surrounding community. The training allowed me to overcome my shyness, and allowed me to find a passion.

I've interned at APHCV for approximately a year and a half. The director of the internship program allowed me to stay longer than the standard three-month program that was offered because they sensed my enthusiasm for the cause. For the past year, it is my responsibility to conduct meetings every week at the clinic and to figure out ways to outreach to our surrounding communities about health-related topics. I am also responsible for training the new peer mentors. During the early meetings I noticed that the new recruits were unusually quiet and shy, though they had brilliant ideas on how to outreach and promote the clinic. I had to coax them into giving their input and feedback to the rest of the group. I saw a part of myself in them because I remember being nervous and self-conscious about my ideas and not wanting to share. By interning at the clinic, I was able to find my voice and develop confidence in my opinions and ideas.

Prior to my internship, I thought I was just one person in the midst of many, and my say-so was irrelevant. Nevertheless, I grew as an individual throughout the duration of my internship, and realized that one voice was all it took. When we organized workshops among my peer group, I made the decision to hold presentations at schools, and as we assessed the workshops, we realized that many of the students we presented to weren't familiar on the subjects we discussed. Each of our efforts made me realize that based on *my* voice and decision, I informed a large group of students that otherwise wouldn't have known about the repercussions of teen sex, alcohol and drug abuse, and so forth. Instead of succumbing to the timid individual I was so used to being, I used the one tool that I felt was my weapon: my voice; and by interning at the clinic, I was able to utilize it and inform my community on a larger scale.

## ANALYSIS

"How I Found My Voice" depicts a cycle of social change: Carol starts out as a shy student, then finds her voice by helping others, then helps other shy students find their voices so that they too can effectively help. This positive feedback loop is truly an inspiration.

Carol conveys her strong personal connection to the cause to which she has devoted so much time and effort. No one could confuse her with a high school student who logged community service hours just for show. She mentions that she was allowed to intern for much longer than the normal term, an important detail that further underscores her passion and commitment. The way she overcame her shyness is all the more impressive given the lack of support from her parents.

Carol creates an ideal balance between her personal story of finding her voice and her passion and the larger story of the impact she had on the world. After all, community service isn't just about finding fulfillment—obviously, it should also be about providing real, meaningful service to the community. Carol communicates that the kind of service she did was mindfully tailored to create optimal impact: "When we organized workshops among my peer group, I made the decision to hold presentations at schools, and as we assessed the workshops, we realized that many of the students we presented to weren't familiar on the subjects we discussed." Unlike many high school students whose experience of service is naive or simplistic, Carol's experience forced her to engage critically with higher-level issues of how to organize a community and empower young people to reach out to their peers.

Ironically, essays on community service can easily slip into a self-centered mode that is all about the warm fuzzies the applicant got from serving. Yes, college essays should provide some insight into the applicant's character, growth or self-reflection. It's not enough to write a self-congratulatory essay whose only message is, "I did a great thing!" You have to say, "I did a great thing, and I learned something even greater from it." Nevertheless, like Carol's essay, a piece on community service should not focus myopically on what you gained from serving, but should also describe what you contributed by serving. The ideal community service essay covers both internal growth and external impact, something Carol has done with aplomb.

## "Trellises"

**Shelby Newallis**
*Accepted by UC San Diego and UC Santa Barbara*

*Essay prompt: Describe the world you come from and how your world has shaped you*

A PERSON LOOKING OUT OF MY bedroom window would see a garden, full of roses, rosemary, and tomato plants. When I look out my bedroom window, I see a garden teeming with life: I see my mother, the ever vivacious rosemary: I see my sister, the tomato plant, beauti-fully innocent, and I see my father, the rose, genuinely beautiful, but with thorns that can pierce the gentlest of skin. My world is a garden, a garden built on the foundations of hard work, respect, and tradition.

Initially, I was too naïve to see the purpose and value of my garden. As a young girl I did not appreciate nor understand the care needed to make a garden prosperous. Growing up, I assumed that all parents got up early to make their kids breakfast and read them books late at night. I thought every kid was taught to say "hello" to adults when intro-duced and that every family went to grandma's house for Sunday din-ner. Nurtured meticulously, my once barren garden was now blossom-ing. It was the ideals of hard work, respect, and tradition that served as the invisible trellises, supporting the growth of my character and it was my parents who made it possible for my development.

This next stage of my life is what I consider my "age of enlighten-ment" because it was the first time that I had a better understanding of me; I now knew why I enjoyed listening to fifties music. I knew why I always wanted to help my grandma cook. And I knew why I continued my community service though my required hours were already com-pleted. It was so clear! I immerse myself in fifties music because I re-spect the pureness of the melodies, I help my grandma create culinary wonders because I value traditions, and I volunteer because I know it is important to support my community. These are the fundamentals that my parents cultivated in me every day. In the process of my own maturation, I discovered how to assist others in their own personal growth. As a leader at San Pedro High School and with The Assistance League, a national community service organization, I have met people outside my normal environment; and I have made personal connec-tions that have awoken innate qualities. Having organized spirit week at school, which resulted in more participation than ever, I learned that I work well with people. Additionally, I learned that I feed off positive energy when I helped at a local political phone banking station and connected with an eighty-year old woman who only spoke Italian; as I spoke to her in her native tongue, she said I had brightened up her day just knowing that her culture has been shared with today's youth. I am inspired by the people that I have met, and my goal in life is to enhance the lives of others like they have enhanced mine.

I have gotten only a taste of the joys of generosity, a taste that has helped to determine my direction in my life, cultivating a global community by sharing my values. I will know that I have succeeded when I look out my window, wherever I may be, and I see my original rosemary, tomato plants, and roses, prospering; but this time, because of me.

### ANALYSIS

"Trellises" uses the controlling metaphor of a garden as its own supporting structure. After a poetic opening, it sets out a clear structure for the essay and communicates that the themes will be "hard work, respect, and tradition." The rich details in the second paragraph bring Shelby's upbringing and process of self-discovery to life. At the end of the essay, Shelby ties the essay back to its original premise. A well-articulated structure like this is easy to employ in most essays, and it well help keep your work tight and focused. If you find that a statement relating your closing to your opening feels out of place, it might be a sign that the essay has become scattered. Shelby manages to include several different topics—her childhood, her relationship to her family, her community service—all within a unifying framework.

She works in examples of her community service experience without sounding preachy—no small feat. Her secret for accomplishing this effect is including a simple, specific anecdote about an eighty-year-old woman with whom she formed a connection. This small example packs much more punch than more generalized statements like, "I discovered how to assist others in their own personal growth." The sentence about The Assistance League could benefit from more specificity about whom exactly she met "from outside [her] normal environment" and what sorts of "personal connections" she made. In a short essay, however, there is probably not space to include vivid examples from each of the activities she mentions. One strategy to deal with this issue in a college essay is to write a draft with examples for each activity you might want to mention, then go through and delete all but the few activities that have the strongest examples. These quibbles aside, Shelby clearly conveys her genuine interest in helping others—the most important hurdle to clear in an essay about service.

Shelby does a particularly good job of giving credit to her family and others in her life for helping her become a better person. She shows that she has moved beyond the childish mindset in which she took for granted all the love and hard work invested in her upbringing to the understanding that cultivating "gardens" takes unflagging care. Instead of merely listing her own positive qualities, she describes how these qualities have developed and matured thanks to her interactions with other people. That is, Shelby's orientation toward learning from others filters into the way she describes herself in the essay. The way she expresses herself—through an essay that is about her, but also fundamentally about the people who have shaped her—is consistent with her stated interest in "enhancing the lives of others like they have enhanced mine." The uniformity of form and content reinforces the sincerity of her statements about her other-focused mentality.

## "Whitney"

**Sumaya Quillian**
*Accepted by UCLA and UC Santa Barbara*

WHEN I THINK OF THE AFTERNOON I met Whitney, I remember how insecure I felt. I feared she would resent me or dislike school, but above all, I was terrified that I would fail her. Fortunately, I decided I wanted to become a tutor for School on Wheels before fear entered my mind. School on Wheels is a non-profit organization that provides volunteer tutoring to homeless children and children in foster care. At the tutor orientation, I quickly noticed I was the youngest person there. I was an inexperienced fifteen-year old amidst a group of adults, and at that moment anxiety began to plague me.

My dad had to supervise my tutoring sessions because I was a minor, but even with him at my side I still felt vulnerable. As I walked up to Whitney's foster home for the first time, I was oblivious to everything except my own nerves. Then the front door swung open, and a fifteen-year old with a huge smile was there. Her greeting was polite and brief, "Hi, I'm Whitney. It's so nice to meet you." Somehow, those words were the first thing to give me relief.

I have tutored Whitney every week since our first session in June 2010. Even though I only spend an hour with her each week, I feel that we have experienced so much together. We have been to college fairs, we have seen museum exhibits, and we have talked about everything from school to family and friends. Some sessions are challenging; we have to review the same subject repeatedly until she fully comprehends it. While those days are productive, I love it when she does not have much homework and we can just talk. I listen to her plans for college, her ever-changing career interests, and lessons she learned in school. From the beginning, Whitney has been willing to learn and to improve, but now I hear how much she wants to learn and how much she wants to achieve.

When I started tutoring Whitney, I assumed it would be a one-sided relationship. I thought that I would be helping her and teaching her. After only a few months of tutoring, Whitney's social worker told me how much Whitney admired me and how much she had learned. I could not help smiling when he told me, because I had no idea how much I would learn from Whitney the first time I walked into her house. She has taught me so much about patience, understanding, gratitude, and hope. Above all, she reminds me how much I love to learn. Looking back, I understand why I was sure that I wanted to tutor Whitney even when I was afraid. I knew that I wanted to help someone learn to love school and knowledge as much as I do. Initially, I could not imagine having an impact as a tutor, because I did not know if I would be good at it. Now I realize that being there for someone who needs help is powerful enough on its own. Every week that I tutor Whitney teaches me that as long as I am willing to learn and help others learn, I will grow and become a better human being.

### ANALYSIS

Sumaya starts her essay with a vivid evocation of her feelings: she builds upon her nervousness in the first paragraph, which the audience is able to share thanks to the feeling of suspense Sumaya creates by giving very limited context at first. In fact, even once we are given the context of tutoring with School on Wheels, Sumaya adds the detail of being a fifteen-year-old among mostly adults, and we become even more nervous—we too share Sumaya's irrational relief when we finally meet the long-anticipated Whitney.

When Sumaya talks about her actual experience of tutoring, she focuses, surprisingly, not on the academic side of things. She talks about going to museums, of just chatting, of preferring the days when Whitney has no homework—the academic part of tutoring is almost an afterthought. It becomes clear through Sumaya's quick description of their tutoring sessions that the relationship is not, as Sumaya expected, particularly academic or one-sided—even before Sumaya says it. It's obvious that Whitney is benefiting from the tutoring when she discusses her "ever-changing career interests, and lessons she learned in school," and when Sumaya makes the wonderfully smart distinction, "From the beginning, Whitney has been willing to learn and to improve, but now I hear how much she wants to learn and to achieve," but it is also clear that Sumaya is engaged in this process of learning. "I thought I would be helping and teaching her," she says, "Initially, I could not imagine having a big impact with School on Wheels, because I was unsure if I would be a good tutor. Now I realize that supporting someone who needs help is powerful enough." Sumaya has very cleverly foregrounded the aspects of tutoring that are not academic, which helps us to see the importance of all the non-academic activities and conversations she has engaged in with Whitney.

Sumaya does an excellent job here of showing rather than telling—and of choosing her examples and her focuses so carefully that the audience comes to the same conclusions Sumaya does just before she says it—that Sumaya seems to be getting as much out of tutoring as Whitney, and that the academic part of tutoring is merely one and hardly the most important, facet of their relationship. She contrasts her nervousness at the beginning with the effusiveness with which she discusses what she and Whitney learned together. The choice of a single, focused anecdote of beginning tutoring with her reflections on her progress along the way and after allow Sumaya to focus very specifically on two lessons she has learned or ways in which she has grown—Sumaya doesn't take on all the aspects of tutoring, and it is in this conscious choice that we can see most clearly what really matters to her.

# 8

# FAMILY

## "Her Hand"

**Kris Thompson**
*Accepted by UC Berkeley, UC Davis, UC Irvine and UC San Diego*

MY BREATHING HAD SLOWED. MY BODY was motionless. The indescribable smell of a doctor's room filled my nostrils. I stared into an almost blinding light above me as the emergency doctor hunched over my face. My sense of touch was numbed in my face and body as the anesthetics coursed through my blood. Yet, for some unexplainable reason, I felt her hand.

In my grandmother's backyard, seven years-old, I was playing by the slightly rusting play-set. I jumped repeatedly over the sprinkler; the warm, rays of summer dripped with the spraying water on to my face.

"Be careful Kris. Don't poke out an eye!" yelled my mom, across the yard.

I brushed off the advice and continued to gambol about my newly discovered fountain of youth. The tree root stood protruding from the wet soil. I never saw it coming. I fell and cut my eyebrow on an exposed nearby screw missing my eye by less than an inch. Globs drip from my brow and splatter on the cement as I walked to my mom.

She had rushed me to the hospital. She had pressed the cloth against my eyebrow as we waited for the doctor. As the doctor stitched me up, the warmth of her loving hand overcame the anesthetics.

Thank you mom, I love you.

I leave you this impression of me: no matter what the situation, the ones I love will always have priority.

## ANALYSIS

Kris starts on a remarkably abstract note—almost cinematic in its presentation, vividness and out-of-sequence timeline—but he manages to drive home exactly and in fact quite forcefully the point that he wants the reader to know about him, to make a statement about Kris' own personal priorities above all else: that Kris, like his mother, will drop everything for and will be fiercely protective of his loved ones.

Not only is this an essay that manages to merge a thoughtful personal reflection, but it is also extremely striking for its vividness and the deftness of its structure. Kris hurls his reader into the scene, into Kris' younger self's own shoes: we are as disoriented as Kris was as we, without knowing the cause or the circumstances, feel his paralysis, hardly able to see for the glaring bright light, passively drinking in the scent of the doctor's office, numb and unfeeling. We can even feel the touch of his mother's hand like an anchor in our sea of disorientation.

Kris puts the reader in his own younger self's shoes so skillfully that he already has our sympathy. Only then does he reveal the premise: we can imagine (with a forewarned shudder) the rusty playset and feel as "the warm, rays of summer dripped with the spraying water." His description of his fall is disgusting, gory, stomach-turning—which is unpleasant to read but delightful in its descriptive richness. Kris deftly ties the end of the story to the beginning of his essay, ending the essay in the same place where it began—with the touch of his mother's hand.

With short, forceful phrases, Kris drives home his point, letting us know with the ferocity and force of his cadence and sentences the ferocity and force with which he will come to the aid of and defend his loved ones.

## "My Name"

**Hayley Ritterhern**
*Accepted by UCLA and UCSD*

*Essay prompt: Describe the world you come from and how your world has shaped you*

MY LAST NAME IS ONE OF those names that people dread reading aloud for roll call, announcements, and any other contact they may have with it printed on a page in front of them. I've seen interesting variations, from Ritterhem to Rittahorn. Although it can be annoying to correct people every time, I embrace the unique name I have, because of the story it represents.

Everyone's mother has a maiden name, and my mom's was Ritter_____*. But oddly enough, my dad has a "maiden name" as well. His was Hernandez. After my parents married, my mom moved here from her native country of the United Kingdom. While she originally adopted my dad's last name, she was the only child of her family, and her own ailing father was sad to see Ritter_____ die. In the spirit of newlyweds striking a compromise, a solution was reached. By combining the first parts of each of their last names, Ritterhern was born.

That blending of a piece of their culture and family heritage has been connected with me my whole life, the first generation recipient of their organic creation. "Ritterhern" summarizes who I am as a person from my Chicano side to my British side, my scientific approach to my love for all things humanities. A descendent of my British immigrant mother, I hold dual citizenship in both the U.S. and the United Kingdom. My father's Hispanic background embraces me with years of deep-rooted family tradition that traces all the way back to my great-grandmother's hacienda in Sonora, Mexico.

Born into a name that itself represents compromise, I embody reasonableness. For example, my friends Katie and Steven stand on opposite sides of the political spectrum, and in our Model United Nations class, I sit between the two, which leads to heated crossfire, as in their debate on the ever-controversial topic of Obama's healthcare plan. Listening intently to the escalating argument, I finally decided that enough was enough. As I cleared my throat, they both stopped mid-sentence. I then spent twenty minutes explaining where their differences arose from, and why each should at least understand and respect the other's opinions. When asked what my own opinion on the topic was, I could argue both sides equally; in the end I'm a strong mediator.

Remaining as devoted to equality and harmony in the world around me as my parents were in maintaining peace in their families, I too become a bridge between differences among friends, the community, and the world in which I live. I am a product of my parents, yet like their last name, I have gone beyond normal expectations to become something new and something great.

This leaves me proud of my name and all that it represents of the merging heritage of my family and of the world which I come from. I know without a doubt that I will not need to correct the reader at the graduation ceremony in four years when he or she announces: Hayley Ritterhern, loud and clear!

\* Name has been abbreviated for privacy.

## ANALYSIS

Although this essay is about what makes Hayley different, it starts by relating to the reader. "My last name is one of those names that people dread reading aloud for roll call, announcements, and any other contact they may have with it printed on a page in front of them." Many people with unusual last names can empathize with this sentiment. Hayley engages those readers with verbiage that is both descriptive and comical. She then admits that her name isn't just different; it was also made up, derived from the last names of both her parents. This fact adds an interesting twist to the story, urging us to continue on.

Admittedly, Hayley benefits from having an interesting story to tell. The origin of her last name is unique. Still, this story alone would not make a strong college application essay. What makes Hayley's essay stand out is its ability to extract significance from this story and use it to explain why her last name describes who she is.

For example, the second paragraph of Hayley's essay notes that the names were combined because the cultural heritage of each of her parents was important to her family. In order to preserve that cultural heritage to the next generation, both names were used. Hayley then continues to stress how her British and Chicano heritage have affected who she is, apart from her name.

Still, Hayley finds more than just cultural meaning in her name. She recognizes that the creation of her name is also a symbol of compromise. Hayley notes that just like her parents were able to compromise with her name, she has inherited an ability to find compromises to conflicts arising in her life. Hayley's fourth paragraph is devoted to exploring this connection, specifically discussing how she finds a middle ground between conflicting ideas in school.

Although well written, more detail could have made this paragraph even more comprehensive. For example, Hayley points out that the debate between her two friends in her Model United Nations (UN) class was about the Obama healthcare plan. However, when describing the argument between her two friends, Hayley fails to mention what arguments each person made, and how Hayley was able to find connections between the two. It is true, that too much detail here would have led the essay away from the main point of the paragraph, Hayley's ability to compromise. However, giving just one example of each side and explaining how she was able to meld the two viewpoints would have more effectively illustrated how Hayley mediated the conflict.

Hayley finishes her essay nicely by reiterating the significance of her last name. The line "I have gone beyond normal expectations to become something new and something great," is especially powerful. With it, Hayley takes ownership of her identity and stresses how her knack for creative compromise can benefit a college's freshman class.

## "Stories"

**Anonymous**
*Accepted by UC Berkeley, UC Davis, UCLA, UC San Diego and UC Santa Cruz*

*Essay prompt: Describe the world you come from and how your world has shaped you*

MY FAMILY IS ONE OF UNKNOWING storytellers. Since my brother and I could talk, my family has gathered around a table every evening, weekday and weekend, to tell stories. We talk about our daily happenings, the gossip we've heard, or the latest political/economic crises to arise. But from my family I've also heard other stories, far more fascinating than the daily goings-on of suburban living; stories that captivated me, enthralled me, consumed me, and changed me; stories that have shaped my life and the dreams of my life to come.

My grandfather, the son of Hungarian Jewish immigrants, would tell us about his childhood in the Bronx, and I'd close my eyes, imagining myself sleeping on a cot in the kitchen of a tenement apartment. I would picture his stories in my mind, trying to envisage the world he had known—his memories had awoken in me a desire to experience a life and a time that was not my own. I wanted desperately to know what life was like in the past—what my own life might have been, if I had been born decades or centuries earlier. My grandfather's recollections cultivated and nourished this fascination with history.

From my father, I gained a world view: the globe expanded in my mind through the many accounts of his travels. Egypt's pyramids, Venice's Grand Canal, Israel's kibbutzes, Mexico's Chichenitza, all materialized in my mind through his words. I would sit for hours at the table, completely spellbound, listening to him describe the different cultures he had visited. From these stories stemmed my voracious traveling appetite—I wanted to see what these cultures were like with my own eyes, experience the food for myself, and learn about the traditions and the history firsthand. My father's travel stories imbued in me a thirst for the understanding of different cultures and places.

My mother's stories offered an entirely different perspective. From her I learned of my Colombian heritage and all the relatives that came with it—my 5 aunts, my twelve cousins, and my very large extended family all played starring roles in her stories. I learned about the Novena, how we pray nine nights before Christmas; I learned how to dance to Colombian music; and I learned how to participate in three different conversations, listen to two others, and eat dinner at the same time. But I also learned how to stay connected to my family, even across continents. Although I don't see my Colombian family often, each time I do it's as if no time has passed. From my mother's stories, I learned that family is a safety net to fall back on, no matter the time, place, distance, or inconvenience.

Stories such as these have shaped my life. Whether they engender in me a love of history, of travel, of family, or some other passion, I always listen with the same thrilling comprehension that I am learning something new, and that this new information will influence the person I will become.

## ANALYSIS

Application essay prompts are intentionally left vague: "What is your "world"? How do you "come from" it? What does "shaped" mean? And shaped from what to what?

One of the most effective writing strategies involves taking the prompt and then defining the keywords specifically for the focus of essay: you. Not the world you think the admissions officer wants to see, but the world *you* live in and how *you* believe that world has contributed to *you* becoming who *you* are today. "World" can be defined as:

➢ a country, state or neighborhood in which you grew up

➢ an ethnic or religious group to which you belong or belonged to

➢ a favorite movie, piece of literature, a genre that you or another created

➢ a culture of sports, art, music, etc.

➢ a daily routine

➢ a way of seeing / interpreting the world

The writer of "Stories" immediately defines her world as her family and all the stories and connections they share with each other, tells us she's been shaped by those stories and family gatherings and then dedicates three separate paragraphs to illustrate three specific family members, their stories and what the writer has learned from them.

The writer uses her grandfather's stories of growing up in the Bronx to show her interest in history and her ability to visualize and empathize with others across time (generation), and space (small urban tenement as opposed to her own comfortable suburban upbringing). Her father's stories have sparked a wider view of the world and have instilled a curiosity and interest in others. Her mother's stories are the writer's main connection to her Columbian heritage and family and tie back into connections over time and space.

All of the topics and values the writer discusses in her essay—making connections between academic subjects and the people in your community, are great especially for an admissions officer looking to populate a univers-"city". However, there are several ways to make the essay even stronger, starting with the beginning: what better way to start an essay on stories than to tell a (short) story? Each paragraph about a family member should also include as much information about the writer (the real subject of this "story"): what history does she like and why? What does she want to do with it? Where has *she* traveled?

Humor is an important element of the essay, but make sure that it's intentional: her appetite might have travelled around voraciously, but she probably wanted to convey her voracious appetite for travelling. (Proofread, proofread, put it away for a day, proofread, have a friend or three proofread, proofread it again and *then* submit it in the application!) Fortunately, the writer shows that she does have a sense of humor when she writes, "and I learned how to participate in three different conversations, listen to two others, and eat dinner at the same time."

And that leaves us with an image of an active, energetic participant in all that's around her.

## "Learning Family Style"

**Anonymous**
*Accepted by UC Berkeley and UC San Diego*

*Essay prompt: Describe the world you come from and how your world has shaped you*

I ORDERED MY FOOD AND THE waiter walked towards my sister. I reached over for my niece's menu and helped her order food while her mom poured over choices. I turned the kid's menu over to hand it back and saw a drawing. For a five year old, it was complex—butterflies around all of us outside enjoying the purple sky. Surprised at her color choice, I asked her why she would color the blue sky purple. She responded, "Why can't it be purple, it is my sky—isn't it?" My five year old niece taught me that my world is a place where coloring the sky purple is more interesting than coloring the sky blue. I learned something that night at dinner, just as I do every anytime I'm with my family.

Dinner is how I learn. My family crowds around the table and competing conversations grapple for my attention. I usually find an excuse to ask my brother a question, and he digresses into a tangent about Lincoln's fights with Seward or Washington wearing his military uniform to the Continental Congress. My brother has shown me that I enjoy connecting the random facts of history together with causes and effects that give these events meaning and purpose.

Eventually, my sister asks how my Biology class is going. She is a scientist who loves to take what I learned one day and connect it to what I've learned every other day. She taught me that education does not begin or end, everything you learn comes from somewhere and is going somewhere else. You learn about derivatives so you can advance in physics, you learn about Chemistry so you can appreciate Biology. Real learning is connecting the seemingly unconnected; something my sister does with every question she asks me.

Learning isn't about facts I can dish out at rapid fire speed, it is about having something to talk about. I engage my family at the dinner table like I engage my teachers in a classroom and my friends at lunch, with a curiosity and vitality that has cultured a love of learning. I am constantly expanding what I know so I have more people to talk to, and more things to talk about. My world is a place where anyone—five year olds, bio-chemists—can teach me anything. In my house, being eager to learn simply means you are eager to talk. I understand that college means coming out of my bubble and entering new worlds, but I will never leave behind what I have learned from the dinner table.

## ANALYSIS

The writer of "Learning Family Style" cleverly frames and constructs his essay around the topic of his essay: the structure, support and strong relationship of his family. He opens the essay showing the whole family together and then spends time on specific family members, giving specific examples of not only how they relate to the writer but also how each influences the writer's interests, worldview and attitude towards education.

Notice how the writer presents family members in a logical progression: seeing the world through the eyes of a child, listening to the older brother's wellspring of historical facts, making cross-discipline connections with the scientist sister. Not only does the writer show how well educated his family is and how close-knit they are (It doesn't hurt that a key indicator of an applicant's potential success at a university is his or her family's level of education), but the essay structure also shows that the writer understands the progress and development of his own education, as well as *shows* that he knows how to cleverly structure and write an essay without saying "I can write well."

Part of the success of the essay lies in the writer's use of specific, concrete examples to support his claims: his niece's purple sky, his brother's stories of Lincoln and Washington, his sister's active involvement in connecting Chemistry and Biology. A subtle sense of humor doesn't hurt either, as when he plays off the dining theme when defining learning as not "about facts I can dish out at rapid fire speed." The writer then takes his "Family-style Learning" experience and connects it to both his academic and social worlds in which he actively and enthusiastically engages his teachers and friends.

The essay could have benefited from the writer showing what interests he, himself, pursues on his own initiative and what he contributes to the table. He admits that he needs to come "out of my bubble," but what does that mean? Ending on an enigmatic note might give a reader pause, so at least he returns to his strength: his family and his love of learning.

### "My Life Saver"

**Jaimie Copprell**
*Accepted by UC Berkeley, UC Davis, UC Irvine, UCLA, UC Riverside, UC San Diego, UC Santa Barbara and UC Santa Cruz*

*Essay prompt: Describe the world you come from and how your world has shaped you*

I COULD NEVER GET AWAY WITH throwing out a toilet paper roll. It always seemed as if the rolls reappeared out of the trashcan into a box for safekeeping. It is silly to imagine someone saving something like this, but in my family, it is routine. Growing up, my dad instilled in me the notion that everything has a use and "If you haven't used it at least twelve times, it is not trash worthy." For years, I have watched my parents save plastic zip-lock bags, outlet extensions, old t-shirts—nothing ever got thrown out. I will admit that my parents' obsession to save irked me at times. I was particularly embarrassed on the days I arrived at school with my lunch packaged ever-so-conveniently in a plastic bag labeled with either "Food 4 Less" or "Auto Zone." As a result of my parents' stinginess, I never owned a real lunch box.

As a teenager, I resented this thrifty lifestyle. But, I soon realized the wisdom behind my family's conscientious saving. To my parents, any item saved, no matter how random, holds a value incomparable to any other. Every hour of work and ounce of sweat they put forth is to earn a living, not only successfully, but efficiently as well. In my life, I have saved it all, reused it all, and found nothing ordinary about my family. Normally, families shop on a regular basis for necessities and luxuries. But, when you have twelve five-gallon buckets of laundry detergent in the garage, like my family does, that sort of shopping is unnecessary.

Since I was a kid, my friends were always teasing me about how well-off my family appeared and how we "have it easy." But, little did they know, such appearances were born out of frugality and careful saving, and my friends just never truly appreciated the circumstances. Money is simply used differently under our roof. Compared to all the houses on our street, we are the only ones with no lawn to water, no cars from later than the 1980's, no air-conditioning, and, heaven forbid, no cable TV. I have lived this way since I was born. Instead, my family saves on day-to-day expenses and adapts to a simpler lifestyle that involves, among other things, conventional television channels and ceiling fans. From this, I have learned to obtain the most I can out of limited resources and that I do not need to own the biggest, newest, fastest anything to be happy.

Living simply has taught me to adapt to any circumstance and that no obstacle can prevent me from living the life I desire. I want to seize every open-ended chance I get to acknowledge the beauty of the world; I want to breathe it all in and appreciate more of what life has to offer, no matter how minuscule or insignificant it may seem. To me, to succeed is to value every aspect of life and to absorb everything I can from it—and I could not think of any better example for that than my family. My dreams of attending the University of California remain high, but my interests lay in the simple things in life. I never needed a lunch box. But, what I could use right now is a trusty toilet paper roll—which, by the way, makes a most worthy pencil holder.

## ANALYSIS

Jaimie's essay combines a sense of humor and intelligent retrospection in her essay about trying to understand her family's thrifty lifestyle. The opening paragraph is charming. We empathize with Jaimie, watching her innocently throw away a toilet paper roll, just to have it magically reappear. The second sentence beautifully couples Jaimie's sense of frustration with her curiosity as to why things in her home were the way they were. These same sentiments are echoed later in the paragraph when Jaimie gives a laundry list of the types of items she was forced to save, and when she recounts the embarrassment she had to feel when bringing her lunch to school in obviously recycled bags. The key to this intro paragraph is Jaimie's tone and imagery. The audience gets a clear idea of the type of life Jaimie led through illustrative examples. We sense Jaimie's frustration, but her language is not overpowered by emotion. Clearly, Jaimie has matured enough to objectively reflect on these experiences, pointing out both their absurdity as well as their value.

In the second paragraph, Jaimie moves away from the well-defined images of what the "world she comes from" looks like, and instead starts to discern the significance of this world. Jaimie points out that although her family "saved it all," each item used in their house had "a value incomparable to any other" new object. Jaimie could have gone even further, naming what the value added was—be it monetary value or the value of supporting a more environmentally sustainable lifestyle. Still, Jaimie's ability to observe the impact of her parents' decisions shows great astuteness for a high school senior.

The next step in Jaimie's essay is important. Many students focus on the world they come from specifically, but Jaimie takes her essay a step further by showing how the world of her family, compared to the world of those around her. In the second paragraph, Jaimie makes a sweeping statement, noting "normally, families shop on a regular basis for necessities and luxuries." These types of blanket statements should be avoided in college essays, because they make assumptions about other people. However, Jaimie corrects for this in her third paragraph when she compares her families' lifestyle to the other people on her street. By observing that her family doesn't have specific commodities, such as a cable TV set, when every house on her street does, Jaimie makes the point that her family's lifestyle is in contrast with the "normal" life standards in her community. This approach of using specific examples and objective information is more compelling and ultimately more effective than her former blanket statement.

In the end, Jaimie ties together the essay by bringing back the powerful images of the lunch box and the toilet paper roll from her first paragraph. The difference is that now Jaimie understands the use for these objects, and embraces their utility. In this way, Jaimie proves that she was indeed shaped by the world she comes from, and she retains the wisdom of the lessons she learned.

## "Hot Showers and River Baths"

**Brian Tashjian**
*Accepted by UC Berkeley, UCLA and UC San Diego*

*Essay prompt: Describe the world you come from and how your world has shaped you*

I HAVE ALWAYS CONSIDERED MY WORLD to be a sheltered one. I grew up in an extremely stable family with two parents and two sisters that have always loved me unconditionally. I have been privileged with a comfortable home and financial situation, and never once has a meal or a house to sleep in been in question. The uncertainty was never whether a meal would be served, it was only which meal would be served. Yet despite spending my entire life with the family I have in the United States, I come from two homes. In the summer of 2010 I was lucky enough to travel with the AMIGOS de las Américas Immersion Program, spending a month and a half in Nicaragua, working with the community on health related projects and lessons in school. It was here I found my second home, the small town of Bajo de los Ramírez, and it has become as much a part of me as that sheltered life that I have been living. Six weeks, as opposed to seventeen years, never seemed like enough time to become part of an entirely new family, but the amount of emotion I felt, (the love, the sadness, the excitement, the fear), proved that wrong. I did not realize how attached I had become until my Nicaraguan father wrote me a letter that he gave to me on my last day in Bajo. As he handed me the note, he looked me in the eye, and with both of us holding back tears, he told me, "Estarás mi hijo, para siempre:" "You will always be my son."

I come from two worlds. I come from hot showers and river baths, queen beds and cots, carpets and dirt floors, clean sheets and mosquito nets, learning and teaching, English and Spanish. I come from loving mothers, hard-working fathers, goofy siblings, dinner with friends and family, conversations about anything and everything, card games where it doesn't matter who wins, impossible goodbyes, and increasing desires to return. These families have shaped me into who I am today and the experiences I have had with both families affect how I plan to live my life. The love my United States parents have shown me for seventeen and a half years has helped me discover how important it is to me to be a father when I am an adult. The hospitality I received from my family in Nicaragua has encouraged me to travel in college and beyond graduation. Finally, the time my United States mother has spent talking to me about being a doctor and the application of those discussions in Bajo while taking care of an injured community member have helped me realize my desire to take care of others for the rest of my life, specifically in the field of medicine. Two families can be too much for some people, but because I have such strong relationships with both, I am very comfortable loving Mom, Dad, Mamá, and Papá.

## ANALYSIS

Brian's essay is interesting because he talks about how six weeks he spent abroad make up half of the "world he comes from." Although Brian doesn't actually come from Central America, by defining his experiences in Bajo de los Ramírez as the "world he comes from," Brian suggests that his short time there has helped define who he is. It is a clever way of illustrating the impact of his time abroad.

The bulk of the essay focuses on the attachment that grew between Brian and his host family. This is most potently done in the anecdote about how Brian's host father said goodbye. His sentence— "as he handed me the note, he looked me in the eye, and with both of us holding back tears, he told me, 'Estarás mi hijo, para siempre:' 'You will always be my son.'" —beautifully illustrates how close Brian and his host family became. This is a perfect example of the "show, don't tell strategy." Instead of Brian claiming that he became close to his host father, he tells a story, using the host father's own words to describe the nature of their relationship.

Although the relationship between Brian and his host family is heartwarming, it doesn't tell us much about who Brian is as a person or as a student. Furthermore, Brian instead of spending time developing what his time in Nicaragua was like, Brian slowly gives us glimpses of what he remembered. His series of comparisons, "I come from two worlds. I come from hot showers and river baths, queen beds and cots, carpets and dirt floors, clean sheets and mosquito nets, learning and teaching, English and Spanish," is powerful and poetic. Brian shows how the luxuries he's known at home lie in harsh comparison to the way of life in Bajo de los Ramírez. Furthermore, Brian discusses these differences with a fondness that alludes to his cultural sensitivity. Instead of discussing how difficult it was to not have hot showers while working abroad, Brian suggests that he embraced the chance to take "river baths" and broaden his experiences.

Brian could have spent more time focusing on what he specifically took away from his abroad experience. Instead he simply states that he learned to see life from multiple perspectives. Brian suggests that moving forward, he will consider the perspectives of both his biological family and his host family when making decisions and continuing his education. He exemplifies this point best when he starts discussing how both parties affected his ambition to become a doctor. He notes that his biological family encouraged him to pursue medicine and gain a higher education, while his time with his host family encouraged him to travel and help others. These details finally give the reader a strong sense of who Brian is within the context of the world(s) he comes from.

# 9

# HERITAGE AND IDENTITY

## "My Tri-Lingual Origins"

**Edward Shafron**
*Accepted by UCLA*

I UNDERSTAND THREE LANGUAGES.

The first of these is obvious: English. Or, more specifically, American English. This language comes from the world that most frequently influences me—that of a high school student in Southern California. This is a world of suburbia that my parents chose for me; of occasional adventures, true—but mostly of routine and comfort. I don't scorn this existence; I thoroughly enjoy living it. In this world I have the time and resources to do what I like—bike, run, and swim to my heart's content, pursue my education, and travel around with my friends. Here I find most of my dreams and aspirations: after proving myself, I strive for the same emotional and personal stability that I have enjoyed in Southern Orange County. The values and mindset I formed here are only a part of the world which informs me, however.

My second language is German. This is something I have learned through three years of study at my high school. This brief cultural exposure—and some travel I have done in Europe and the Pacific—has served to add a certain international awareness to my dreams. I have begun to appreciate the vibrant world outside of my current sheltered existence, and this is something that I want to experience further.

My text-book German is different to the German that my grandfather learned during the Second World War. He learned grudgingly and out of necessity as a Ukrainian prisoner to the German Army, in a deadly world where uncertainty and struggle were as regular as the sun rising.

After the war, through wit and will, he made his way to Australia, where my father was born. And through my father, I was taught courage, intelligence, and humility. In this way the world of my grandfather has influenced my dreams and aspirations –his world is also mine. I aspire not only to the materially attainable, but also to personal integrity and character.

Now my grandfather had to learn a new language, that of Australian English, to get by in his new world.

Thus my third language and the third facet of my world—Australia—the country of my birth.

Australia is a less tame world than Southern California. The Australian stereotype—of a loud, adventurous, bronzed people—is well deserved. This is a country obsessed with sport, where the family and the physical are two of life's sacraments. I discovered the reward and enjoyment of a "bush walk", a rugby game, and sense of caring family felt around the "barbie". My dreams always include this aspect of my world—a life where I have a warm, happy family and healthy lifestyle.

My three worlds are inextricably intertwined and spill over into each other. They will continue to shape my dreams and aspirations as they evolve over time. But my "tri-lingual" origins will stay with me, and I hope that I can do justice in my life to the ideals represented by each.

## ANALYSIS

This essay combines some extremely deep introspective insight with a well-crafted, almost poetic structure. Edward organizes his essay around the linguistic influences in his life and ties those linguistic influences, and the history from which they come, to the elements that define him and his experience.

This is an incredibly skillful, artistic way to integrate Edward's family history with his diverse life experience, his language skill and his hopes for the future, all while showcasing a very smart sense of literary organization and a command of a high-level vocabulary.

Edward begins with a hook—an impressive assertion about his abilities, although in itself not particularly unique. But when he begins with "American English" as his first language, we can see that this essay is certainly not going to be about Edward's achievement in high school language class. We can see that he is appreciative of the relative affluence in his life, but introspective about it, and that he keeps it in perspective compared to his family's origins. This section allows Edward a little bit to showcase his other extracurricular activities and his well-roundedness.

But where the essay really takes off is when he leaves off of high-school German class and points out, "My text-book German is different to the German that my grandfather learned during the Second World War." This juxtaposition, and Edward's clever embedment of his third language into the story of his grandfather, launches the essay into a completely different territory: Edward's intriguing family history and his strong connection and identification with it and his father and grandfather shows the stark contrast between Edward's own suburban life in Southern California and his family's past struggles through wars and emigration. But Edward, by delineating and showing us the values he has received from his father and grandfather, reinforces the sense of what he says, that his grandfather's "world is also mine." We see Edward in a completely different light, and the very care with which he tells his family's story reinforces the sincerity with which he asserts his values, his care for his family and his constant introspection and assessment of his surroundings and background.

Edward writes with skill, and more importantly, he writes with care and sincerity. Certainly, he has life experience and privilege of his own, but the vividness, specificity and generosity with which he forefronts his father's and grandfather's struggles is remarkable and likeable, and the skill with which Edward ties his values, ideals and goals to a specific set of experiences and family memories associated with the linguistic influences in his own life is admirable.

**"Transitioning across Diversity Lines Effectively"**

**Linda Thai**
*Accepted by UC Berkeley*

*Essay prompt: Personal quality, talent, accomplishment, contribution or experience*

THROUGHOUT MY LIFE I'VE BEEN EXPOSED to a variety of languages, specifically Cantonese, Mandarin, Teochew, Khmer, Vietnamese, Spanish, and English. Due to my family's past experiences with the events of the Khmer Rouge, they frequently relocated to different areas near Cambodia and acquired new languages and dialects from other Asian countries. As a child, I constantly dealt with transitioning between Teochew when speaking to my parents and English with my brothers, while also learning Khmer through observation. Due to my exposure to several languages at the time, I became overwhelmed and shied away from crowds, not wanting to speak up fearing that I would speak improperly and be shunned upon. However, transitioning between these languages would eventually strengthen my multilingual communication abilities and comprehension skills with a diverse range of people. With the privilege of being familiar with four languages today, as a young child, I wouldn't have guessed that language would have such a significant impact on my life.

During family gatherings when I was young, my relatives conversed in a mixture of Chinese, Khmer, and English; it would catch my attention, and I would turn and listen attentively to try to figure out what was being said. Having such curiosity as a child, I didn't back away, I remained close by because I wanted to learn the languages too. As I became older, I occasionally went to Chinatown with my mother, which provided another opportunity to listen to conversations and observe social interactions. Repeating my actions as a child during family gatherings, I would listen, but this time I thought of the cultures and traditions these strangers shared with each other and the similarities I shared with them; that we are victims of social injustices, political underrepresentation, economic inequalities, and personal challenges. These strangers, bound by similar social injustices in our society, caused me to think in depth; as humans, many tend to focus more on the differences of people rather than their similarities resulting in a lack of appreciation for each other. Understanding this offered me a sense of comfort and gratitude for the different cultures and ethnicities in the world because, whether it's tradition, culture, music, or food, these factors bring our society together while maintaining global diversity. Through this ongoing experience, I've learned to appreciate the differences in every person because the distinctiveness of each individual also works to establish bonds between them. This quality gives me a sense of pride because I've learned that with differences come commonalities.

Thinking about my interest for languages makes me realize that as individuals born into a world of diversity, we are exposed to such a limited amount of it. My experiences with different languages make me proud because I'm able to keep an open mind and to understand and relate to more people, which inspire me to develop my sociability skills. I was known to be reserved when I was younger, but I've become more gregarious as I familiarize with different languages, cultures, and people and the social injustices we experience.

## ANALYSIS

Linda's story about how she learned seven languages tells us a lot about who she is both as a student and as a person. Of course, Linda's language background speaks to her immense cultural knowledge. Throughout the essay, Linda mentions that by learning how to speak with people from different countries, she was able to in turn learn more about the world. This, along with the fact that Linda moved so often as a child, suggests that Linda is both cultivated and adaptable. Linda's knowledge of global customs and issues comes up over and over again throughout the essay. When Linda discusses how she was able to relate to strangers about "social injustices, political underrepresentation, economic inequalities, and personal challenges," the reader gets a sense of Linda's sensitivity to those around her. This awareness of other people, their lives and their cultures allows Linda to grow from both her own experiences and the experiences of the diverse set of people who surround her.

These details give a lot of information about how Linda developed into the person she is today, but her process of learning Cantonese, Mandarin, Teochew, Khmer, Vietnamese, Spanish and English talks to who Linda is as a student. Throughout the essay, Linda discusses the various learning styles she employed to pick up several different tongues. Some languages she learned through traditional means, mainly speaking to her friends and family members. Other languages she had to learn by observing other people or just listening, both of which are significantly more difficult. By mentioning these various means of educating herself, the reader gets a sense of how resourceful Linda is. The fact that she made the effort to learn additional languages, through her own effort, demonstrates Linda's sincerity and willingness to learn.

This enthusiasm for learning also shows through when Linda discusses her personal nature. At first, it seems that Linda is intimidated by the diversity around her. She notes that she "became overwhelmed and shied away from crowds, not wanting to speak up fearing that [she] would speak improperly and be shunned upon." One would think that this would prevent Linda from picking up new languages in turn. However, Linda does the opposite. Instead she leans close to hear the conversation happening at her family dinner table and embraces the chance to go to the market where she can pick up new words or phrases. These scenes in the essay again speak to Linda's enthusiasm for learning. In turn, Linda's keen interest in understanding the world around her turns her into a more outgoing person.

Linda's final paragraph wraps up the essay perfectly as she realizes that learning to speak seven languages is more than just a skill. It is a process that has brought her the world knowledge and the social confidence that define the person she is today. Linda's ability to outline how this process created this effect is what makes her essay ultimately so effective.

## "The Freedom in My Origins"

**Cristina H. Mezgravis**
*Accepted by UC Irvine and UC Riverside*

*Essay prompt: Describe the world you come from and how your world has shaped you*

JUICY TURKEY, GREEK SALAD, WARM "HALLACAS" (a traditional Venezuelan dish), Latvian ginger cookies . . . . Sounds mouthwatering, no? These are some of the dishes that sit on the table at my traditional Christmas dinner, reflecting the hybrid of customs that exists in my family. My maternal grandparents are Greek and Latvian, and my paternal grandparents are Venezuelan. Diverse backgrounds are the yin and yang of my character, but, together, they shaped my aspirations in a unique way. Thanks to them, my vision of happiness involves two key elements: being surrounded by the laughter of my relatives and having nothing to hide.

Both sides of my family have played an instrumental role in the formation of my character, but, most importantly, they taught me the value of family. When getting to know me, you find yourself facing a layer of courtesy and prudence chiseled by my father's side: you have to dig anything personal out of me with a spoon, but this means I am just getting to know you better. I have never seen a problem so incendiary as to make my father raise his voice, and, similarly, I seldom get mad, but I don't recommend trying to wake me up on a weekend. In contrast, I have seen my maternal relatives cry listening to an old song. I guess that's why it's normal to catch a glimpse of a tear rolling down my cheek during a movie. As in a typical Greek family, *everybody* is in *everybody's* business and though this can be frustrating at times, from them I've learned to understand that "my problems are their problems," and I've tasted how comforting it feels to have people who will help you up when you fall or simply give you a comforting hug—a feeling that once tasted is indispensable for the rest of your life.

I learned the importance of honesty from my grandfather: I remember cocking my head to one side and gazing at him while he told me, "There is nothing more rewarding than going to bed with a clear conscience." While this view of openness and forthrightness has always been the European core of my family's teachings, a noticeable characteristic of Venezuelans is their caution: you can find yourself talking to one for hours, but if you analyze the conversation, you'll notice that it didn't get past politics or gossip.

Although the European side advised me to be honest, my father, as a Venezuelan, juxtaposed this idea, "You count true friends on one hand, and you'll have leftover fingers." I was once naïve enough to trust everyone who surrounded me, until I found myself facing their backs. I'm not proud to admit that each time I hit this wall, I grew increasingly bitter at people around me, until the day when Jaime Jaramillo, a globally recognized social leader, defender of children's rights, and probably the most inspiring individual I have ever met, gave a speech at my school. I found that a few of the characteristics I despised, I displayed myself. I had a total change of perspective; instead of being disappointed every time I was slapped by reality, I could choose to look at the positive in an individual and treasure the few individuals who had my back.

I felt relieved to finally find how the European and Venezuelan sides of me could merge into one. Because of the support and love of my family and my dedication to honesty, I learned to believe in myself and finally set aside society's expectations of finding a supposedly lucrative career, and opted instead for honesty with myself by pursuing a Major in what I love: Creative Writing. Figuring out where I was from, literally and metaphorically, has freed me to find out who I will be.

## ANALYSIS

The essay starts by detailing the food present during Cristina's "traditional Christmas dinner." This first sentence of the essay is enticing; the mouthwatering descriptions capture the attention of the reader while illustrating the various cultural influences that make up Cristina's family traditions. She then goes on to answer the prompt quite literally, by describing how her Latvian, Venezuelan and Greek family members have helped define who she is as an individual.

Cristina organizes her essay by going through each of her notable character traits and pointing out where those traits came from. This structure suits the theme of the essay well. As Cristina is talking about the "world she comes from," (i.e. each of her relatives) she is also talking about herself. In this way, Cristina's essay answers the prompt, and yet never ventures too far off from the purpose of the prompt, getting to know more about Cristina. Furthermore, Cristina's descriptions of both her family and herself are well developed. Instead of simply listing each characteristic and who she learned it from, Cristina helps the reader understand what each character trait means to her. For example, instead of simply saying that her Venezuelan relatives are cautious, Cristina explicitly describes what the word "caution" means in the context of a conversation. In Cristina's eyes, having "caution" means never venturing beyond a shallow discussion of "gossip or politics" when chatting with peers. In this way, we learn that Cristina's definition of caution also involves some kind of social awareness. These definitions are unique, and they further aid our understanding of Cristina as a person.

Unfortunately, the structural organization of Cristina's essay begins to break down in Cristina's fourth paragraph. She loses focus on her family and its influences. Instead, she vaguely describes how she used to trust people too much and "found [herself] facing their backs." Without further discussion of what "facing their backs" means, Cristina then thanks "a globally recognized social leader" for helping her understand how to value more supportive individuals. Although admirable, this paragraph doesn't quite fall in line with the rest of the essay, which focuses on how her family helped form her into the person she is today. This paragraph would have complimented the essay more if Cristina had given more details about what happened and explained how her family's definitions of trust and friendship helped her re-consider how to choose friends.

However, the final paragraph of the essay brings the essay back on topic. She notes that by understanding her family, she learned to understand herself. In turn, she was able to come to terms with why she wanted to pursue her potential major. In this way, Cristina nicely ends the essay. We walk away with a strong sense of who Cristina is because of her family, but we also gain an understanding of who she intends to be apart from them.

## "Passion and Potential"

**Nhi Yen Nguyen**
*Accepted by UC Berkeley, UC Davis, UCLA and UC San Diego*

*Essay prompt: Describe the world you come from and how your world has shaped you*

AS I LOOK ACROSS THE BURNING pavement, I see a flurry of colors in motion. Ascending, descending, and transcending the depths of my pride, I applaud the young girls behind the umbrellas.

Having grown up in my Vietnamese community, I am delighted to be involved with all the facets of my culture. In the school where I learned my native language, studied my country's history, practiced my religion, and found support in the encouraging arms of family and friends, I established my roots in Vietnamese dance.

Participating in the annual holiday shows is always a momentous occasion. After each performance, my girls scurry over, seeking my approval. When they recognize my beam of motherly pride, they smile with a sense of accomplishment that can only be exceeded by my own. As a choreographer and dancer, I know that preparation and practice are essential. With every song selection, costume change, and prop placement, my perfectionist nature sets in, only to be whisked away by my passion for the process.

The rhythmic flow of the dance form coincides with my gentle nature, yet its sharp precision balances with my free spirit. Creating the routine and guiding its artistic direction allows me to utilize the full potential of my creativity. However, nothing can compare with my joy in teaching my girls. By focusing on their unique talents, I ensure that the cohesive effort is a perfect blend of synchronization, vivacity, and enjoyment. Over the seven years of dancing, I have learned so much from my peers and mentors, and by incorporating their experiences with my personal taste, I have developed and grown as a performer, gaining confidence and social understanding.

Naturally, I am extremely ambitious: I do not fear the impossible. My culture is such a big part of who I am, so I want to reach out to my native country. In the future, I hope to travel back to Vietnam and do all I can to help the country rise out of poverty. A place where children yearn for a pencil, the poor resort to stealing toilet paper, and the hungry commit suicide to end the pain should not exist. To amend the atrocious situation, a cooperative and compassionate community must be established.

Although I have yet to bring my full plan to fruition, I have made progress through community service. Nevertheless, my ultimate goal is to give all people the necessary tools to develop self-sufficiency. Whether on stage or off stage, I aspire to enrich the lives of others and myself. With the resources of a higher institution to strengthen my knowledge and character, I will be able expand my impact in the global community.

## ANALYSIS

Nhi immediately lights a fire of interest with her first sentence. Why is the pavement burning? What's the flurry of colors in motion? Fire? Explosions? Riot? She then uses the nifty linguistic trick of tripartite feminine rhyming ("Ascending, descending, and transcending") to shift from the physical ("flurry of colors in motion") to the emotional and personal ("the depths of my pride"). The applause at the "young girls behind the umbrellas" both calms our worry of danger yet still remains mysterious enough to make us want to continue reading. That's quite a bit packed into the first two sentences!

After piquing our curiosity, Nhi then defines not only her world ("my Vietnamese community") but also which aspect is most important to *her*. "I established my roots in Vietnamese dance." Remember that the essay prompts are intentionally vague and open to interpretation, and a successful writer will quickly define the terms of the prompt in relation to him or her while also focusing on a specific aspect of the "world" in which to ground the essay.

Nhi is a successful writer not only because she spotlights the most important aspect of her world to her, but she also *shows* us her world by employing many concrete and sensory details that place us in her shoes: girls scurry over and bask in the "beam of motherly pride," while in the impoverished parts of Vietnam "children yearn for a pencil, the poor resort to stealing toilet paper." She also demonstrates her quality writing ability by employing mature, appropriate diction ("I ensure that the cohesive effort is a perfect blend of synchronization, vivacity, and enjoyment.") and use of alliteration ("With every song selection, costume change, and prop placement, my perfectionist nature sets in, only to be whisked away by my passion for the process.")

All the while, Nhi layers a complex portrait of herself. Not only is she a dancer, but a choreographer as well, with the ability to organize and direct a performance. She works well with kids, and indeed she recognizes that teaching and helping others is more rewarding than the individual joy she feels when dancing herself. This flows directly into and explains her commitment to public and community service, and she connects the dance-hall stage in her local community to the world stage of International Aid. And we can easily see her firm belief in teaching self-sufficiency within herself.

While her concluding paragraph is a bit vague (*what*, exactly, is the "full plan"? We're excited and want to know how she'll put her passion into play!), we definitely come away with the feeling and understanding that this is a person who *will* make a change, and she'll do it with art, elegance and love.

# 10

# HUMOR

## "My Summer Herding Cats"

**Edward Shafron**
*Accepted by UCLA*

LAST SUMMER I HERDED CATS.

Well, that's not entirely accurate.

I would say I led small cougars. That is accurate.

As captain of the Capistrano Valley Cross-Country Team, it was my job to make sure our freshmen cougars (our mascot) were trained and prepared for formal practice when our coach could legally (according to CIF rules) begin his training.

The task was similar to being a shepherd to felines literally, and more.

It meant organizing the 32 novices not only to run in the same direction (a difficult feat in itself) but keeping track of athletes of disparate speeds, and convincing them not to commit the cardinal sin of Cross Country—walking.

I had to provide coaxing when coaxing was required and sharper commands when that was indicated, too. I gave impromptu sermons and delivered anecdotes in an attempt to inspire and assuage.

The exchange of experience was not one sided. Plenty of time was spent fussing over how to best motivate in activities that were hard to complete and easy to slack on, like push-ups. In situations like this, I learned, the carrot was far more effective than the stick.

They grew as runners and I grew as a leader.

I made my blunders. During a practice run through some canyon trails, I alighted upon a pair of freshmen standing uncertainly at the edge of a creek, the path continuing on the other side.

"It's not called cross country for nothing, lads," I chirped as I blithely strode through the stream.

At times I almost forgot that one 13 year old under my care who shuffled along in a pathos-inspiring 10 miler mirrored me—but 3 years ago.

It led me to reminisce to my own time as a novice when each practice was an uncertainty, when you could meet your doom on each 45 minute shuffle. What a journey it had been!

I remembered the Cross Country captain when I was a freshman, and the terror inspired when he, practically a full grown man, told us we were going to be running hill-repeats on a hill called "the beast." The beast?!

I tried to emulate his authority, but also to create my own (new) sense of approachability and friendliness. My self awareness (and self consciousness) was heightened on account of 32 fresh high-schoolers that I had never known before.

Those cats—the Capo Valley Cougars I had under my care—were a challenge to herd. But together they learned to work as a team and I had my first lesson in leadership.

Now approaching the last race for the runners who embarked upon their journey four and a half months ago, I find it appropriate to feel a little bit of pride. Those freshmen are now first place in the Sea View League.

## ANALYSIS

In this essay, Edward writes a rather bold and stylized literary account of his exploits as cross country team captain. His essay is on the more formal and more polished side, and at times his "herding cats" theme may be a little contrived and his affected diction may impede his meaning, but he displays considerable skill in crafting a tightly focused and meaningful essay while displaying a command of rhetoric and vocabulary that in itself is impressive.

As far as the focus and structure of the narrative is concerned, it is extremely tightly focused, and there doesn't seem to be a word or sentence out of place: Edward leads in with a hook—somewhat contrived, but understandable once explained—gives the necessary background information, describes his experiences, his struggles and what he has gained, tying it up neatly to the hook he used in the beginning. Edward's language and expressions, too, are very formally structured, with some sentence components even artificially balanced in pairs of two: "I had to provide coaxing when coaxing was required and sharper comments when that was indicated, too. I gave impromptu sermons and delivered anecdotes in an attempt to inspire and assuage."

Edward's most successful transition in the essay is his moment of reminiscence on his own days as a novice—it comes just in time as he, as the taskmaster, is about to lose our sympathy, and as he himself, in his narrative, is forgetting that he too once struggled. He regains our sympathy and that moment of introspection allows Edward to expound briefly on what his idea of leadership is: coaxing and sharp comments, sermons and anecdotes, inspiration and assuagement, but also friendliness and approachability, tempered by self-awareness—all of which Edward has shown that he displayed in his essay.

This essay isn't without its pitfalls, and the formality of its tone and the contrived structure aren't for everyone, but Edward has the rhetorical skill and vocabulary to pull it off. He is a little weakened by his reliance on cliché—herding cats, stick-and-carrot. His elevated word choice causes him to stumble occasionally: "At times I almost forgot that one 13 year old under my care who shuffled along in a pathos-inspiring 10 miler mirrored me—but 3 years ago" is a difficult sentence to read even the second time around.

Edward tempers these moments and the somewhat ponderous nature of his formal structure and elevated tone with admissions of weakness, confusion and his reminiscences on his own days as a novice—which allows us to see this as a process of growth rather than mere proclamation of achievements. Additionally, Edward is clearly a gifted writer and his choice of a more formal essay allows him to display that—a bold choice that ultimately plays to his strengths.

## "Jerry"

**Jeremy Press**
*Accepted by UC Berkeley, UC San Diego, UC Santa Barbara and UC Santa Cruz*

*Essay prompt: Personal quality, talent, accomplishment, contribution or experience*

THROUGHOUT MY LIFE I HAVE HAD nicknames, but my most recent one reflects my qualities as a person. From years one through seven I was known as "Mookie," from seven through fifteen I was "Jere," and on the baseball field I'm "JP." My most current nickname "Jerry" is the name I hope to carry with me for the rest of my life.

The nickname Jerry was actually a mistake. Late one night over winter break, my friend's mom left the "em" out as she called my name, turning "Jeremy" into "Jerry." At first, only a few of my closest friends called me Jerry, but after a while, the name stuck and now almost everyone I know calls me Jerry. Of course, this was not enough for my friends, who came up with different variations over time, such as "Sweet, Sweet, Jerry" and "Silverback Jerry." (Let's just say I have some unique friends.)

I see myself as private, observant, thoughtful, and logical. I used to have trouble talking openly and expressing myself. I didn't have as many friends as I do now, and with parents who both worked full time and an older sister who didn't want to have much to do with me, I spent a considerable amount of time alone. But as I got older, I developed a more playful and lively attitude with mannerisms that my friends bring out in me. I have also found that my humor has helped me develop closer friendships with people who have lived through a lot and have shared their struggles with me.

Thinking about my friends and their lives has led me to ask myself some tough questions about how I see myself and what is important to me. I have decided that life taken seriously can still be humorous and enjoyable. This is my philosophy in work and play.

However, it is not all deep thinking and personal reflection. The meaning of the nickname still lies mostly in its ridiculousness. The name Jerry reminds me of a middle- aged man with a graying mustache, a bowler hat, and a wooden cane—not a senior in high school. The older Jerry and I have a lot in common, though. First of all, the middle-aged Jerry and I both have a slight limp. (Mine is due to a shortened

Achilles tendon on my left leg; his is due to wear and tear that is normal for someone his age.) Second, we both are known to slap our knee when we laugh. I still do this instinctively despite my friends' playful jests. Third, we both enjoy a Sunday afternoon at Dodger Stadium, although old Jerry would probably reserve the last three innings for a well-deserved nap.

Not to overanalyze a nickname, but this serious and also silly nickname describes me. I am proud that this nickname represents a happier, more open, and more sociable Jeremy. It will me enable me to contribute more and to have a fuller and more valuable experience in college.

---

### ANALYSIS

"Jerry" makes effective use of humor throughout the essay. In keeping with the essay's tone, Jeremy might have been better advised to start off with the lighthearted list of his nicknames, rather than with the rather generic opening statement he uses. As you draft college essays, try out a few different openers. See if you can pull off an opening that begins *in media res* ("in the middle of things"). Sometimes you have to clear your throat, so to speak, by writing and discarding bland opening lines. Thrusting the reader into the middle of a story or a vignette can cut through preliminaries that take up valuable space in a short-format piece. However, you must keep in mind that the goal is to immerse, not bewilder. Make sure you provide enough information for the reader to find his or her bearings before long.

The two shining moments of this essay are Jeremy's discussion of his gradually increasing sociability and the comparison between himself and "old Jerry." They each bring something very different to the essay. Jeremy's discussion of his social development demonstrates that he is a thoughtful and caring young man. He doesn't brag about it, but the reader learns that he is the sort of person that others feel comfortable opening up to. What's more, he is sensitive enough not only to empathize with friends' "struggles" but also to reflect on his own life in relation to theirs. The section on "the older Jerry" complements these more earnest revelations by revealing Jeremy's goofy sense of humor. Introducing an imagined incarnation of his nickname is an ingenious and unusual device. It shows that he has enough of a sense of humor about himself to relish a nickname with connotations that others might flee from as "uncool." At the same time, it allows him to provide several tidbits about who he is without simply ticking them off in a dry list format. The comparison and contrast with his alter ego provides deepens his self-description.

Jeremy's final paragraph, like his opening, treads the border of some essay clichés. His last sentence, especially, is not specific. The line, "It will me enable me to contribute more and to have a fuller and more valuable experience in college," could plausibly be an ending to many college essays. Nevertheless, the final paragraph does fulfill the function of making an explicit connection between what Jeremy has discussed and his assets as a potential UC student. If an essay's content seems obscure or unrelated to college, explicit links like this can be useful. Overall, Jeremy's essay works because he shares who he is and makes the reader want to get to know him.

# 11

# ISSUES

## "Juan"

**Jackie Botts**
*Accepted by UC Berkeley, UCLA and UC Santa Barbara*

*Essay prompt: Personal quality, talent, accomplishment, contribution or experience*

LAST YEAR, I WORKED AS A peer mentor at my school. Mentoring my friend Juan revealed to me the power of education and an integrated support system, as well as my own potential to inspire and to be inspired.

Juan is intelligent, perceptive and inquisitive, but when he puts pen to paper, words scramble and numbers become inscrutable. Poor study habits often overpower his efforts to keep up with his schoolwork and he rarely expects to succeed; but when he does, his smile says it all.

Juan was selected into the Academy, a group of 30 at-risk students taught by DPHS's best teachers and peer mentors. The results have been remarkable: grades increased dramatically while discipline referrals dropped. The students were held accountable for their education, some for the first time in their lives. They were expected to succeed. For the first semester, I mentored several students in the Academy's US History class, and second semester I also worked one-on-one with Juan in his Guided Studies class. My job was to role model strong study habits, keep Juan on-task, and provide him with as much support as possible. It was tough, but within a few weeks, he'd shown me that he was a kid like me and deserved the support I've always taken for granted.

Juan is one of the 800 students failing classes at my school, but there will never be a mentor or Academy for each one. I came home many days feeling disillusioned. Invariably, however, Juan would soon prove me wrong. He would get a spark in his eye as he connected an English article on racial-profiling to his own life, recounting with simple eloquence the racism he had faced. More poignantly than any inspirational speaker, he showed me that education can be relevant, personal, and empowering.

Juan will graduate this year and this means much more than one high school diploma for one kid. Juan's diploma will represent the success of the Academy, of his teachers, of peer mentoring, and most of all, of Juan's perseverance. It will also support my belief that positive expectations and unswerving support is often key to student success. I am very proud to have supported Juan as he attained his goals. Most importantly, Juan has taught me how important it is that every student be treated with respect for their value and potential because they are entitled as much as I am to the benefits of an education.

### ANALYSIS

This essay discusses an issue that is pervasive throughout the United States, mainly, the challenges that face underachieving students. Although this issue is widespread, Jackie's ability to make the essay personal is what makes it compelling. From the onset, we get a clear picture of Juan; he is "intelligent, perceptive and inquisitive, but when he puts pen to paper, words scramble and numbers become inscrutable." The reader makes a connection with Juan and empathizes with his need to learn, just as Jackie gives us hope that he will ultimately achieve his goals. The personal nature of this essay is what makes it unique. Many students write essays about service projects they do in other countries, for a week or two over the summer. However, the work Jackie did spanned an entire academic year and affected members of her school. This is important because colleges want to admit students who are willing to commit to strengthening the community they live in, not just communities abroad.

As the essay develops, there is a clear indication that mentoring was intrinsically rewarding for Jackie. Her lines about how proud she was at Juan's graduation, or the simple statement "his smile says it all," display the joy Jackie felt from doing something she truly believed in. These descriptions convince us that Jackie's dedication to the project was earnest.

Although the essay revels in moments of achievement, it does not steer away from the harsh realities that face Juan. Descriptions of Juan's challenges show how Jackie is cognizant of the problems such as racism, low expectations and lack of support that face at risk students. Jackie proves that she is willingly aware of problems that face her community, even if they do not directly affect her. This shows that Jackie is insightful.

In her fourth paragraph, Jackie admits that there will never be enough help for every student in her school, which is again insightful and realistic. Impressively, instead of being pessimistic about the little impact she may have, Jackie commits herself to making a difference in any way she can. She finds a way to use the skills she does have, in order to help those around her. For example, like many strong students, Jackie possesses "strong study habits." However, instead of being the only benefactor of her study skills, Jackie models her study habits for other students so that they can achieve academic success as well.

By the end of the essay, we know Jackie was a mentor, modeled study habits and provided support for Juan, but we still don't know much about Jackie's involvement in the Academy. There is no clear narrative of how she got involved as a mentor, the specific challenges she faced, or what she plans to do in the future to help enriching the lives of her peers. As the reader, we'd like to learn more about Jackie. We can only assume that Jackie's earnest enthusiasm for mentorship will encourage her to continue helping the members of her community after high school.

## "A Home Without a Home"

**Ali Cardenas**
*Accepted by UC Berkeley*

ECOLOGICALLY, A COMMUNITY REFERS TO A group of interdependent organisms interacting with one another in the same region. However, humans are one of the most complex species to inhabit the earth, with their ability to not only process, but react to, emotions, through empathy. This ability to understand and acknowledge the suffering and elation of complete strangers is what separates mankind from the animal kingdom. In society's terms, a community is much more than simply living beings making contact with each other; it is working together; helping those in need; feeling for one another.

My neighborhood can hardly constitute society's definition of a community. In fact, it primarily consists of people "interacting" at a bare minimum with each other. There is no sense of unity, harmony, peace. Everyone appears to have been spat out by the universal power of poverty onto a rundown assortment of crumbling houses, and then expected to coincide with one another. There is no community. It is an eat or be eaten world. It is survival of the fittest. It is the animal kingdom.

When I was younger, I did not understand the reasoning behind my parents' warning, "Don't go outside by yourself, Alita." I did not comprehend the sirens and police helicopters I would hear each night, just prior to saying my prayers and being tucked in by my mother. I had no idea that beyond the four-walled haven I call my home, lays a jungle of atrocities: people stealing from the innocent; children being abducted in the dark shadows beneath the glistening moonlight. That is no way for people to live with each other. A community is meant to be a larger family outside the home; but in my neighborhood, along with many other low-income minority areas, one is lucky to exchange glances with a stranger, let alone avoid altercations.

The greatest local issue I continue to face is that my "community" lacks every imaginable characteristic of a socially-thriving community. There is no PTSA; no community council; no embodiment of an extended "family." My neighborhood is an array of various races, cultures, people, yet we are very similar. Many of us have experienced the same struggles, whether they may be financial, educational, or societal. As much as we may acknowledge this well-known fact, we continue to live our lives in ignorance. We lack the ability to bond and empathize with one another. We are already placed towards the bottom of the food chain, so why do we persist in making it harder for ourselves by only further secluding ourselves?

Despite the odds, the expectancies, the statistics that have claimed that I would not even graduate from high school, I have never allowed myself to use my neighborhood as an excuse or limitation for what I can achieve. In fact, I use it as proof of what I can uphold; proof to those who have doubted me, simply because they read a piece of paper with my Hispanic name and address on it.

## ANALYSIS

"A Home Without a Home" shows how effective a controlling metaphor can be. Ali uses the definition of an ecological community to make cogent comparisons with her own human community (or lack thereof). The metaphor is a vehicle for her to describe the problems of the community she lives in in an organized and clever way. Phrases like "survival of the fittest," "jungle of atrocities" and "bottom of the food chain" show her verbal ingenuity and create a sense of continuity throughout the piece. Moreover, it takes serious smarts to sustain a multi-pronged and nuanced comparison.

The examples that Ali describes in her second paragraph make the conditions in her community more concrete, allowing readers a glimpse into day-to-day life there. These details serve as a good counterpoint to the more abstract material in her introductory paragraph, in which she defines what a community should be. After providing a "slice of life" in her neighborhood, she then switches back to a deeper, sociological analysis of what is missing in her community and the perplexing lack of cohesion there. This mutually reinforcing interplay of example and analysis is subtle, but it is one of the major strengths of the essay. Ali shows that she can write well enough to choose evocative details and set a scene, while also demonstrating that she has the analytical sophistication to consider, from a sociological perspective, why things are the way they are. She makes a good choice in posing a question ("We are already placed towards the bottom of the food chain, so why do we persist in making it harder for ourselves by only further secluding ourselves?"), rather than making a sweeping generalization, at the end of this paragraph. After all, a college essay is too short to make a nuanced argument about a hefty issue like this one. There is room, however, to make cogent observations, as Ali does in enumerating the social institutions her community lacks and pointing out the paradox that a group of people with so much in common seem so at odds with one another.

In her final paragraph, Ali underscores a point that is by now obvious: she is not telling this particular story for sympathy. After all, we've already seen how this topic has allowed her to highlight her authorial and analytical abilities and provided insight into her background. *That's* what makes it a good choice for her to write about in a college essay. Her last two lines are a fierce declaration of her admirable determination to transcend the demeaning expectations' others have of her based on her "Hispanic name and address." "A Home Without a Home" is an excellently executed piece that goes above and beyond the expectations for a college essay.

# 12

# LEADERSHIP

## "Leave Your Heart on the Dance Floor"

**Kaitlyn Makanaakua Basnett**
*Accepted by UC Irvine, UCLA and UC San Diego*

*Essay prompt: Personal quality, talent, accomplishment, contribution or experience*

I DO NOT WANT TO DANCE today. This thought runs through my mind as I shuffle to my car, swing the door open, and slump myself down into the seat. It has been another long Monday. I fumble to stick the key into the ignition, start the car, and get out of my neighborhood. I could be sleeping right now; maybe I should just turn around and go home. I get onto the freeway and my limbs continue to force me to drive on, drawing me nearer to my destination while I stress over the AP Statistics homework I have yet to start. My radio drones on as I pull into the parking lot where I park and shut off the engine. I step out of my car and hobble over to the trunk where I grab my skirt and water bottle before slamming it closed. I walk grudgingly towards the front door of the studio. Let's get this over with. My night as a Polynesian dancer begins.

I step into the studio, smiling meekly at the parents as the door jingles shut. I throw my skirt on and tie it quickly as I enter the room where all the girls are waiting eagerly for class to begin in five minutes. They are standing in the center of the dance floor and making sure that their skirts are on just right, using the mirror in front of them to carefully adjust the bottom so that it is the same length all the way around. "Hi Katy!" "Katy's here!" "Hey Katy!" are some of the exclamations that fill the room the second they see me. Their excitement dissipates the cloud from above my head. I guess I do want to dance today.

I spend the next hour with these girls, helping them to learn their techniques correctly as well as understand how to dance with the music. With them, patience comes naturally. I wait eagerly for the grace to click in their young brains, for the music to fill their hearts in a manner that will hopefully make every step like a mere breath someday. I watch as they take in each new movement and try their very best to do it exactly as I am demonstrating it. The glow that surrounds them when they manage to learn a step correctly fills me up with pride. No amount of sleep could ever match this feeling of accomplishment.

I then spend the second hour with girls of a slightly higher dancing ability, helping them to perfect their techniques rather than just learn them. The key is to understand how to express the love of dancing, along with dancing to the music. The glow is much harder to produce within these girls. They know how to dance for the most part, and they dance mainly because their parents want them to. They could be sleeping right now too. I try and treat each of them with the utmost respect, avoiding a condescending tone with them at all times. However, I still find it difficult to produce passion within them.

The studio owner's daughter Malia speaks to the girls at the end of every class. On this Monday she focused on the statement, "Leave your heart on the dance floor." It is truly as simple as that—something I realized. I have become a leader through my passion for this culture. During these two hours of my evening, I help the girls who were once in my place as eager students, teaching them how to dance and how to express their own passions. I instinctively try my hardest to assist them in discovering how to take their heart out of their chest and lay it in front of them on the dance floor. What I feel when I dance is something I try and pass on to my students.

After a long day, Polynesian dancing dissipates the cloud that hangs over me. When I dance, I leave my heart in the process. I forget about AP Statistics and I forget about sleeping. I forget about how long of a Monday I just had. I tell the stories of the Polynesian culture and the values of unity and family through my actions. I walk away from the dance floor feeling free and prepared to take on another long day. I realized on that Monday that whatever activity invokes a passion within us should be highly valued and shared with our peers. I am confident in my abilities as a student and I realized on that Monday that my dream of becoming a Pediatrician is one that will never fade; it never has faded. However, I also want to be a Polynesian dancer and I want to do it forever.

## ANALYSIS

Kaitlyn's essay begins on a tough note. Although beautifully written in a strong narrative style, the tone of the essay closely runs the line between eloquent honesty and complaining. The image of Kaitlyn brooding in her car after a long, hard day, although negative, is something most people can relate to. Furthermore, the fact that she still decides to go to dance class shows Kaitlyn's commitment to her art. Similarly, the scene describing Kaitlyn meekly entering the studio provides a contrast to the image of kids excitedly flocking around her, while she leads them through dance class with a reinvigorated love of dance. Together, these scenes illustrate how dance brings balance to Kaitlyn's life.

The third paragraph picks up speed with a moving description of Kaitlyn's young dance class. Kaitlyn shows both leadership and caring by patiently showing her students through steps. She becomes inspired by their passion to learn; her words— "to fill their hearts in a manner that will hopefully make every step like a mere breath someday" —sound like poetry. As the audience becomes convinced that Polynesian dance is important for Kaitlyn, she acknowledges that teaching kids how to dance is worth more to her than sleep. This establishes a well-developed positive contrast to the tone of her opening paragraph.

Yet, Kaitlyn's description of her second class is not as upbeat. The reader gets to see that Kaitlyn is able to work with students of a higher skill level, but the enthusiasm of the previous paragraph isn't there. Her students are forced by their parents to dance and Kaitlyn expresses frustration in her inability to inspire them. Furthermore, Kaitlyn's mention that "they could be sleeping right not too" mimics her own negative feelings about dance from the beginning of the essay. In turn, faith in Kaitlyn's love of dance is lost.

However, Kaitlyn again re-works the negative tone to prove a point. She hears the studio owner's daughter and is finally able to put words to the lesson she is trying to teach both her classes. Kaitlyn talks distinctively about what it is she loves about Polynesian dance and what inspires her to "put [her] heart on the dance floor." It's not just teaching or dancing that is important to her. Instead, Kaitlyn is also passionate about the cultural significance of her work and how that makes her feel closer to her family. These specifics help us understand why dancing helps her overcome negative feelings she may have for classwork or lack of sleep. Finally, Kaitlyn suggests that her passion for dance is mimicked by her passion for other things, such as pediatrics. Although the mention is brief, Kaitlyn encourages the reader that dance is just one of the many things she loves and strives to commit her life to.

## "The Football Experience"

**Mitchell Brisacher**
*Accepted by UC San Diego and UC Santa Barbara*

*Essay prompt: Describe the world you come from and how your world has shaped you*

THE DIFFERENCES ARE STARTLING EVEN TO me, and I lived it. Looking at pictures and video from my smaller, less athletic freshman days of football, I am amazed at my growth. My coaches have molded me into a football machine. I have developed into a vital piece of a CIF championship caliber team, even though I am not the flashiest or the most recognized player in the Windward football family. When other teams scout us, usually I do not come up on their radar. But I am the team's leader and the glue that holds everything together.

My place in the Windward football community is one of fundamental importance. After winning the 2010 California Interscholastic Federation Southern Section Football Championship, our leader graduated and the team lacked a figurehead. I filled that role like a linebacker filling a hole. With no hesitation, I stepped up as the team's physical and spiritual captain. From leading pregame rituals, to keeping the intensity up in practice, to making the big play when needed, my teammates turn to me for advice and guidance. Whenever there is a question of the team's direction, the team goes where I guide them.

Another aspect of my leadership is treating every player with respect. Every year I take on the "rookies" (freshmen) and integrate them into the community. I try to mentor them so their transition into Windward football is as smooth as possible. My junior year I mentored a quiet freshman, who started off slowly. By the end of the season, under my guidance, he was a heavy contributor to the team. Now he is also one of my good friends, and we can go to each other for advice because of our close bond.

My freshman year we made it to the semi-finals for the first time in school history. Building on that success, we continued to excel and win the CIF Championship my junior year in 2010. I learned from previous years' mistakes to reach the pinnacle my junior year. Instead of ignoring mistakes of the past, I embraced them to better myself, a skill I use regularly.

When the madness and unpredictability of a football game breaks loose, my coaches trust me to lead. I have played every position on the field, from quarterback, to defensive line, to long snapper. My adaptability gives my coaches freedom to move players around, knowing they can ask me to play any position. My adaptability has also transferred to other walks of life, and I carry it with me always.

Being a part of the Windward football family has shaped my dreams and aspirations by teaching me what is possible through hard work. I have learned that I can set my own path and get the success I desire with dedication after seeing how much I have changed while reaching my goals.

## ANALYSIS

Mitchell takes an essay about football and makes it about something much larger. He opens his essay by highlighting the pronounced physical changes he has undergone as he morphed from a "smaller, less athletic" freshman to a senior football player. This comparison ends up being only a point of departure for him to talk about even more important strides he has taken as a leader during those four years. In his first paragraph, Mitchell creates an intriguing contrast between his unobtrusive presence on the field and near-invisibility to scouts and the bold statement that he is "the glue that holds everything together." At the most fundamental level, the essay is an explanation of how Mitchell has developed into a leader through his high school football career. Implicitly, the piece argues that Mitchell's leadership skills, founded on the football field, will serve him well as a UC student.

The essay uses specific details to substantiate the main claim about the author's leadership abilities. The sentence, "From leading pregame rituals, to keeping the intensity up in practice, to making the big play when needed, my teammates turn to me for advice and guidance" does a particularly good job of showing, rather than telling. The list of specific activities is the equivalent of hitting the play button on a football movie montage in the reader's mind. The author also takes the opportunity to include some memorable lines that further enliven his essay. He makes clever use of a football simile to note that he filled a leadership vacuum "like a linebacker filling a hole" and begins a paragraph with the blood-pumping phrase, "When the madness and unpredictability of a football game breaks loose." Sharp turns of phrase like these show that the author has taken the time to finely polish his work, and help stave off the creeping clichés that so easily worm their way into college essays.

At a few key moments, Mitchell makes statements that connect his leadership skills on the football field to his positive qualities off the field. He writes, "Instead of ignoring mistakes of the past, I embraced them to better myself, a skill I use regularly" and "My adaptability has also transferred to other walks of life." It's useful to include a few explicit links like this to connect the specifics of the essay topic to broader conclusions about your character and what you have to offer as a university student, but they need not be heavy-handed. This essay successfully weaves in a few understated connections like these without beating the reader over the head with parallels that should already be obvious.

## "Leadership"

**Armand Nelson Zenarosa Cuevas**
*Accepted by UC Berkeley*

*Essay prompt: Personal quality, talent, accomplishment, contribution or experience*

GOING INTO MY JUNIOR YEAR, I felt a little empty inside: I wanted a leadership position, something that I lacked for the past six or seven years. After finally settling into high school, I wanted to cause change within the student body and make a real difference. I felt my school lacked active involvement in community service, so I looked to the Interact Club.

The Interact Club is an on-campus organization that focuses primarily on community service. Coming into my junior year, I aimed for a top position in the club. I wanted to make a difference and fulfill my ambition to lead. As a member at the beginning of the year, I made my presence noticeable with perfect attendance and active participation in all activities. While members usually averaged five to six hours of service, I had a respectable sum of seventeen by the 2nd semester. My dedication was most prevalent in the Barnes and Noble gift wrapping event, where I worked around twelve hours during Christmas break.

The officers took notice of my hard work and dedication and inducted me as a Member-at-Large officer during the second semester. Within only a few months, I had to prove to the senior officers that I was capable of strong leadership, careful planning, and structured organization. When I was put in charge of the Big Sunday service event, I planned the Whittier Narrows Recreation Area clean-up and the school clothing drive. For the drive, each officer had to bring in some large boxes to distribute around the campus. A few days every week, I drove to Costco to get as many boxes as I could and brought 80 out of 100 total. At officer meetings, I asked questions and expressed my opinions, making sure my voice was heard. As part of the banquet planning committee, I went out of my way to drive 30 minutes to a store to buy cheap seasonal items like leis, bubbles, and umbrella straws to coincide with the banquet's beach theme. As the year drew to an end, I applied for club president. I was very anxious and doubtful whether or not I would get the position; to my excitement, they honorably appointed me as the new Interact president.

I am highly proud of my huge jump from being a simple member to becoming the high-ranking president. The alumni officers and advisors of the club express their pride in me and their belief that Interact will continue its great legacy. Although club president comes with immense responsibilities, I confidently accept these responsibilities, making sure I effectively delegate jobs evenly between officers, thoroughly plan every event, powerfully preside over all meetings, and take utmost care in organization. As president for my first and final year, I pledge to increase participation in Interact and spread a desire throughout the campus to help the community and learn what our motto, "Service Over Self," really means.

## ANALYSIS

Armand's essay is called "Leadership," but instead of discussing his leadership talent, it illustrates his ability to identify and fulfill a goal. By focusing on why he wanted to become president and what he was able to do to achieve that position, the reader learns about Armand's work ethic and commitment to service. Both these qualities in turn make a good leader.

First, Armand identifies why he wanted to become leader of the Interact Club. He explains that his motivations were both to gain the opportunity to try leadership and to improve the amount of community service being done at his school. Armand's ability to identify the needs of both himself and his school demonstrates perceptiveness. His ability to fulfill both those needs simultaneously demonstrates his efficiency. Furthermore, by providing his own train of thought, Armand gives the reader a sense of his motivations as well as his decision making process.

The essay then walks through the steps Armand took to earn the position of president. Specific examples of his actions in the Interact Club show how he was able to stand out from his peers. For example, the essay states that "while members usually averaged five to six hours of service," Armand far surpasses that average by putting in 17 hours of service in a single semester. By giving exact numbers and a benchmark average, Armand uses objective data to support the claim that he worked hard and was dedicated. Similarly, Armand discusses specific sacrifices he made, like going out of his way to get materials for an event. These examples demonstrate Armand's desire to consistently work hard to pursue his goal, even after gaining some short-term success by being named a Member-at-Large officer.

Finally, we learn that Armand's hard work paid off; he achieved his goal of becoming Interact Club President. This fact is most notable because Armand had to be appointed president. Therefore, much like his appointment to "Member-at-Large officer," other people had to recognize Armand's achievements and agree that he deserved to be appointed. This fact confirms that Armand's presidential position was well earned.

The final line of the essay importantly clarifies what Armand plans to do, now that he has become President of the Interact club. His goals for expanding the membership and impact of the club demonstrate that as a leader, Armand is forward thinking. His ambitions to progress the club are commendable. More importantly, having just demonstrated his capacity to pursue and achieve a goal, the reader is assured that Armand can successfully progress the Interact Club and the impact of its service.

# 13

# PERSONAL GROWTH

## "Bass Lake"

**Amber Fearon**
*Accepted by UC Berkeley, UC Davis, UC Irvine, UCLA, UC Santa Cruz and UC San Diego*

ZOOMING DOWN THE LAKE WAKEBOARDING HAS always been one of the best memories of my family's annual vacation to Bass Lake. Unfortunately this summer, my younger cousin, Nick, tried a freestyle jump and his wakeboard gashed his forehead open. I looked back from the boat to see blood, mixed with lake water and tears, gushing down the side of his face. Without hesitation, I jumped into action. I yelled to my aunt to quickly throw the safety flag up and turn the boat around, while instructing Nick to grab the rope so I could pull him in. Once we got Nick into the boat and wrapped in a towel, we raced home, where my aunt immediately rushed him to the hospital.

After docking the boat and cleaning up Nick's mess, the shock of what had happened hit me; I realized how over the years my role in our family trips to Bass Lake had clearly changed. Ever since I was three, my dad's side of the family has spent this week of summer together, enjoying water sports and each other's company. I started out as a young passenger wedged between two adults, wearing my puffy, yellow life jacket and covered in a mound of damp towels. Without even noticing the transformation, I'd grown into a watchful and mature leader, constantly making sure that everyone is safe in the water and on the boat.

Although I loved Bass Lake as a carefree child, motivated by fun and play, I love it even more as a conscientious young adult. I am able to lead my little cousins by example, and use teamwork with my family to make boating and water-sports safe and enjoyable. By seeing how my family cares for one another, I have learned more about them than I ever thought possible. Having time to relax with my parents removes us from the ordinary, busy routine, and has allowed us to become extremely close. Enjoying the company of my family while making crafts, talking, and playing in the water reinforces our strong family bonds. This Bass Lake tradition has imparted on me vital life lessons, while leaving a lasting fondness for experiences that I know I will share with my own kids someday.

## ANALYSIS

Stylistically, Amber manages to make much of a short answer. She doesn't spend much time in the beginning with background, giving just the essential setting of wakeboarding. Instead, she begins *in media res*: Nick is bleeding within the first the sentences of the essay, and Amber is leaping into action with no discussion of forethought or in fact any thought at all. Amber perfectly shows rather than tells how her love for her family, time spent bonding with them and caring for her cousins has conditioned her into becoming, as she says, "a watchful and mature leader, constantly making sure that everyone is safe in the water and on the boat."

She further stylistically mimics the sequence of events by reflecting on the event only after the crisis has passed and Nick has been rushed to the hospital: "After docking the boat and cleaning up Nick's mess, the shock of what had happened hit me." Amber transitions seamlessly from a display of artistic writing to her critical analysis of the incident's effect on her, which allows her to showcase in this essay both her writing skills and her own reflections on her maturation. By the time she recalls herself as a "young passenger wedged between two adults, wearing my puffy, yellow life jacket and covered in a mound of damp towels," the readers are already drawing a comparison in their mind between the young Amber and the one we have seen leap into action without hesitation on behalf of her younger cousin.

What's more revealing about Amber is not her responsible reaction to trouble, but the fact that she realizes in the essay that she prefers spending time with her family in this role to her carefree younger days. Not only, then, does Amber tell us that she is responsible and quick-thinking, but she also prefers to play roles in which she needs to be exactly that. This revelation shows great maturity and great introspection, and Amber makes it clear how her new role as a responsible caretaker in the family heightens her appreciation for the uninterrupted time she gets to spend with her family on vacation.

Finally, Amber looks to the future: superficially describing herself looking after her cousins, she foreshadows herself returning to the lake with her own children. But more importantly, she offers the sense that she will bring not only her responsible and sensible acumen to other aspects of her life in the future, but her power of introspection as well. She covers a lot while focusing on one single but demonstrative event.

## "Potential to Contribute"

**Stephanie Anderson**
*Accepted by UCLA and UC Santa Barbara as a transfer student*

AS OF LATE I HAVE TAKEN great pride in my ability to bridge the gap between people, and with this I will try and unify the student community at the University of California. I am able to relate to people as a result of lessons I learned in the time I spent living and traveling abroad, as well as because of my varied interests.

In the Spring a couple years ago, I lived in Spain while attending the University of Granada. I also travelled around the continent, visiting Italy, the United Kingdom, Holland, Germany, Hungary, and the Czech Republic. While being exposed to different cultures, I also learned to relate to others and to be open to new ideas. I worked to gather some information about the people in every country I visited, and tried to pick up basic vocabulary such as "Hello", "Goodbye", "Please" and "Thank You", even in countries where I knew many people would speak English. While I would visit the museums and monuments throughout the day, at night I would try my best to visit local haunts, in order to see the real people at the heart of every location, rather than the plastic tourist side. These efforts made me aware and considerate of the people around me. As a result, I formed lasting friendships with people in various countries.

In addition to what I learned in Europe, I also find it easy to relate to others as a result of my varied interests. I am deeply passionate about a wide array of music, from Blues to Punk to underground Hip Hop. I love film, and I am as entertained at an independent film as a well-written Hollywood blockbuster. I am fascinated by art nouveau, I keep updated on politics and world affairs, am a food snob, wine lover, and I will not hesitate to let my inner geek out to play. I enjoy myself if I am outside playing a pickup game of Frisbee, snowboarding, or just running around. On the other hand, I will have just as good a time holed up inside just talking with a friend. I can talk sports with the boys or drool over shoes with girlfriends. I speak fluent Spanish, poor French, and random bits of Italian, Dutch, Berber, and Czech, and a lifetime of avid reading has resulted in my knowing plenty of odd bits of information.

All of these things have helped me to get along with a wide variety of social groups. This extends beyond people my own age. Anyone who sees me interacting with children tells me I would be a wonderful teacher. On the other hand, others are often impressed with how well I get along with adults much older than myself. More than that, I have been able to bring people from different backgrounds together. When I get my friends together, there are people of varying ages, nationalities, and interests. Given the chance, I would love nothing more than to demonstrate my gift for communicating with my peers and relating to the world around me at the University of California. I believe the University will benefit from accepting me as those like myself thrive off of other strong, charismatic and interesting individuals. I hope to add flavor to the campus body while unifying and expanding it, nourishing myself and those who I am fortunate to meet.

## ANALYSIS

Writing about how you will contribute to a college can be truly daunting. Some students find themselves stumped, unable to imagine what they alone can offer to a campus of thousands, out of a pool of thousands of applicants. Others feel uncomfortable—or far too comfortable—tooting their own horns. In this essay, Stephanie does not offer particularly unique experiences, although hers are broad and varied, nor does she offer a particularly artistic essay, but she avoids the common pitfalls of selfishness and self-aggrandizement that this topic can engender, and instead she frames her contribution not in terms of what she herself brings to the table but what she can offer to those around her.

In terms of structure, Stephanie keeps it very simple and straightforward. Rather than beginning with artistic anecdotes, flashbacks or some other narrative device, she treats her essay as exactly that—an essay. She offers in her introduction a thesis of sorts: she notes her "ability to bridge the gap between people," and posits that "with this I will try and unify the student community at the University of California." She moves on to explain the origins of her ability to mesh comfortably with people from all walks of life, countries and identities, beginning with her extensive travel experience and her unique attitude to travel. She then cites evidence of her ability to move fluidly from disparate groups of people: from underground hip hop fan to snowboarder to wine snob to girly-girl, she offers us an engaging and energetic picture of herself as comfortable in situations that are as diverse and varied as Stephanie's own interests and enthusiasms are. She finishes the essay with a concluding argument in which she sums up the gist of her essay with a few illustrative examples: "Anyone who sees me interacting with children tells me I would be a wonderful teacher. On the other hand, others are often impressed with how well I get along with adults much older than myself. More than that, I have been able to bring people from different backgrounds together. When I get my friends together, there are people of varying ages, nationalities, and interests." Then she finishes on a strong concluding claim: "I believe the University will benefit from accepting me as those like myself thrive off of other strong, charismatic and interesting individuals."

Certainly there are more artistic and less direct means of addressing this topic, but Stephanie's forthrightness and simplicity allow her unique and uniquely unselfish take to shine through. Stephanie evokes her varied and wide travels, her knowledge of foreign languages and her long-lasting friendships with people she has met on her journeys not because she can bring these experiences with her to UC campuses and thus enlighten others with her knowledge and wisdom. Rather, she feels that she can facilitate meetings and ultimately friendships between her fellow students who, being inevitably incredibly diverse, may otherwise never have met and thus never been enriched by bonding with people radically different from themselves. Where many students would write only about themselves, it is apparent that Stephanie has at the front of her mind the welfare and enrichment of the community around her: it is not that she herself will be an enriching friend to them—although she likely will—but that she can and wants to facilitate bonds of friendship between the people around her. Many applicants have had wide travel experience; many have made lasting friendships with an astonishing array of different kinds of people; many will write more creatively structured essays—but Stephanie is memorable and especially likeable because of the generosity, genuine enthusiasm for community and self-effacement without excessive or affected modesty or self deprecation inherent in her argument.

## "Leave It to Me"

**Amber Fearon**
*Accepted by UC Berkeley, UC Davis, UC Irvine, UCLA, UC Santa Cruz and UC San Diego*

OVER THE LAST FEW YEARS I have babysat to have some extra spending money. As the summer after junior year rolled around, I began talking to my parents about my financial situation, including earning and saving money for college. I realized that I had the perfect job with families living in my neighborhood. To build my business, I made and distributed fliers, posting them at local elementary schools and the community center. Soon after, the phone was ringing constantly with neighbors asking me to baby-sit. Before I knew it, my job had expanded to include watching over people's houses, gardens and pets. My baby-sitting job had rapidly evolved from a three family operation to successfully taking care of twenty plus families all over Lafayette. By working hard to be punctual and develop a strong relationship with each family, I was able to strengthen my recommendations and further increase business.

I am incredibly proud that "Leave It To Me", my expanded summer enterprise, became a huge moneymaker in just three short months. Although I have had to reduce my hours while school is in session, I've continued to serve my neighbors whenever my schedules allows. With an extra period free this semester due to district budget cuts, I have been able to reallocate more time to my clients and continue to save money for college.

Creating a business taught me about offering a valuable service, setting up the right marketing, working hard and managing my time well. I now have a better understanding of the importance of saving and budgeting my money. Making my own business took motivation, perseverance and determination in order to keep my connections current and business expanding. The massive amount of time I put in was made worthwhile because I learned important lessons about starting and building a business.

········································································

## ANALYSIS

Shorter-answer essays don't allow much room for creativity and artistry, which many students find to be a struggle; at the same time, they shouldn't just be a prose version of what's already visible on your application. Amber here manages to successfully communicate what she has learned from her business venture, how it has changed her and how she might apply these lessons to her future, but she manages to tell a story that is organic in its evolution and personal in its details.

Amber begins her narrative with the background and inspiration for her business: like many other teens, she babysat, strategized with her parents to earn money and planned how to save for college. But when Amber says "I realized that I had the perfect job with families living in my neighborhood," we hardly expect her to launch into her description of what she did to "build my business." This abrupt and unexpected transition communicates Amber's decisiveness and her efficiency, both of which clearly contributed to the success of her business. She echoes stylistically the rapid growth of her business with the ascending list: "Soon after, the phone was ringing constantly with neighbors asking me to baby-sit. Before I knew it, my job had expanded to include watching over people's houses, gardens and pets. My baby-sitting job had rapidly evolved from a three family operation to successfully taking care of twenty plus families all over Lafayette."

Amber's attention to detail is not only welcome to the reader, making her specific and memorable, but it also serves to suggest yet another reason why Amber's business acumen is so successful. She pays attention to small but important details like punctuality and makes it clear that she puts respectful and accommodating relationships with her clients first.

Amber's summary of what she learned in the last paragraph doesn't necessarily include claims of life-changing experiences, but its specificity makes it particularly genuine. She admits that she's pleased that it is a "huge moneymaker," and we appreciate her honesty. "Saving and budgeting," "managing time well" and "offering valuable services" may not be revolutionary discoveries, but their down-to-earth nature and their specificity, as well as Amber's efficient and clipped style, give the reader the sense that Amber has taken these lessons to heart. Rather than being let down by the vagueness of the formulaic ending "I learned important lessons about starting and building a business," we get the sense from the preceding content of the essay that Amber genuinely has not only learned these lessons but has applied them successfully to her own life, and will do so to future ventures.

## "The World I Come From"

**Jeremy Press**
*Accepted by UC Berkeley, UC San Diego, UC Santa Barbara and UC Santa Cruz*

*Essay prompt: Describe the world you come from and how your world has shaped you*

THE WORLD I COME FROM HAS been shaped by my connections to people. The people that have impacted me most have been my family, friends, and my baseball team. These people truly make up the world I come from. The first group that has affected me is my family. My family has taught me to be hard working without taking myself too seriously. My Mom specifically is always joking around with me and giving me a hard time for being a teenager. For example a few years ago she clipped out an ad from the *Los Angeles Times* that read "Happy Mother's Day! We love you so much. David, Tom, and Annie." My mother crossed out the names from the ad and wrote Anna (my sister) and Jeremy instead. She then promptly put the clipping up on the fridge and it remains there today, many mother's days later, stuck behind a magnet in the shape of a cow. My parents taught me to be self sufficient. They taught me to be responsible and independent. For example, instead of sticking their noses in my academics, they gave me space with the expectation (but not requirement) that I would excel. This has required me to make the conscious decision to stay motivated at school and to make my own successes.

My friends are also a very important part of my world. Since entering high school I have become close friends with a group of guys that have impacted my life greatly. Before I got close to these friends I used to feel up tight and anxious during my day. My friends are always helping me loosen during a stressful time in my life. My friends have also taught me to laugh at myself and to see the lighter side of things. This is most prevalent right before first period every morning. We congregate outside the library to catch up and crack jokes before class. This helps me start my day with the right attitude and allows me to focus during class. An example of their impact happened recently during a fifth period English class right before lunch. In the middle of our discussion on *Hamlet* the school's fire alarm blasted off and caused me react by jumping in my seat. A few of my friends noticed and we all started laughing in unison. In previous years this would be a very negative experience for me and I would consider classically embarrassing, but what I will remember is the joy that my friends and I got out of the situation.

My baseball team is also a very important part of my world. Playing on the baseball team is where I have learned about commitment and perseverance. I have learned that it is not always about being the best but participating in something greater then myself. Our team puts commitment and effort above talent and that has taught me a lot about life. From this experience I know that the most important thing is that I feel I have done my best and put my efforts toward an important goal with people that matter to me. I find it interesting that the baseball team at my school has more practices than any other team, but also has the most fun. The people in my world have taught me that the most important thing in life is to do something that you love and to not stop doing it.

### ANALYSIS

Jeremy's essay makes good use of vignettes that bring to life the joy of ordinary moments in his life. The humorous tone of the essay shows that he has taken to heart his family's advice "not to take himself too seriously" and his friends' positive humor influence. The offbeat example in the first paragraph about his mom's appropriated Mother's Day clipping disarms the reader with its sheer oddness. Although it may not register on a conscious level, the mention of the "cow magnet" adds to the wackiness of the story and demonstrates the power of including a well-turned detail. Details like this can add pizzazz to the dangerously dull genre of the college essay.

Each paragraph in this essay makes its own coherent argument, supported by a relevant incident in Jeremy's life. The first paragraph makes two points: the author's family taught him to have a sense of humor about himself and to be self-sufficient. The others make one point each, an appropriate level of simplicity for a college essay. Trying to get too many points across can dilute the power of a short essay, especially when it becomes impossible to provide effective support for each one. The simple, clear format that Jeremy has chosen allows him to pair a vignette or observation (such as, "I find it interesting that the baseball team at my school has more practices than any other team, but also has the most fun") with each major point. By the end of the essay, the reader can piece together the points to learn that Jeremy is humble, self-sufficient, able to laugh at himself with friends and committed to his endeavors. Including examples from his home life, social life and an important extracurricular activity makes Jeremy seem well-rounded.

This is a great example for students who worry that their lives aren't "exciting" enough for college essays or who feel like they have nothing to write about. This essay uses everyday events as its raw materials. Jeremy isn't writing about a traumatic life event or the time he climbed Mount Everest, but his essay stands out from the pack because it has the authentic sound of his own voice. Thanks to that voice, readers finish the essay with the sense that they have gotten a true glimpse of his personality—and it's an appealing one.

## "Knowledge is to Know Nothing"

**Danish Qasim**
*Accepted by UC Berkeley*

THE SUFI MYSTIC IMAM AL-GHAZZALI ONCE wrote that a man can attain half of knowledge by the realization that he knows nothing. I came to such a realization one year ago through the humbling experience of being stumped by a nine year old girl who asked me a seemingly simple question. She inquired, "If our lives are predetermined by God, why do we have to do anything?" This question could not have come at a better moment in my life as I had just finished giving a presentation on Islam at a local Methodist Church as a part of my outreach organization's efforts to bring religious tolerance in the community. Immediately after giving a well received presentation, and after being overcome by feelings of pride and scholarliness, I was forced to reconsider, because the little girl's question and my subsequent embarrassment helped me understand the point of the Imam.

I realized the nature of knowledge is comparable to the universe, the more we learn about it, the more cognizant we become of our insignificance within it. I was able to easily answer questions of jurisprudence and scripture, but I had no answer for the most relevant question concerning my existence. As a result, I made a commitment to study not just Islam, but a variety of religions. I began intensely studying the Arabic language in order to attain a proper understanding of the Quran, a scripture of unparalleled linguistic beauty. This increased my understanding of God, as I learned Arabic allows for us to speak about God outside of time, through the omission of words such as 'is' and 'was'. My quest has taken me many places from academic institutions such as churches and universities, to places of social consciousness, such as, homeless shelters and orphanages. As a full fledged philomath, I have been enrolled in over ten hours of weekly extra-scholastic classes for the past two years, including comparative religion and Islamic apologetics. I have also studied with internationally renowned theologians at the famous Zaytuna Institute in Hayward, CA.

I discovered that all the religions I studied call people to embrace the highest qualities within themselves, such as intellect, and to overcome their lowly aspects, such as greed and envy. This made me realize that religion itself is a beautiful system meant to honor humanity through understanding and tolerance, but it is only its practitioners who give it a bad name.

As a result of my dedication to religious studies, I have gained recognition from my peers. I have been invited by many high school clubs to speak at their events and offer religious guidance to students. Currently, I volunteer as an instructor in a Sunday school, teaching key religious texts to a class of high school students. Ironically, I have found that as my understanding grows, my desire to teach diminishes. Realizing my potential impact on my audience's life, and knowing that an inadequate job can render me a fountain of misguidance, I have begun to exercise extreme caution.

To increase my religious knowledge, I recently went on an exclusive religious and historic retreat to Arabia this summer. I found myself reflecting upon a scriptural passage while reclining in the Holy Mosque of Medina, which read, "Everyone will be rewarded with that for which they strived." Over time, this verse helped me realize that although our fate is determined by God, each person must struggle nonetheless to reach his or her full potential as a creation of the All-knowing, and I believe that admittance to the UC is the missing necessary next step in my personal quest for such potential.

## ANALYSIS

Politics and religion are two topics that are very challenging to use in an application essay, as it is very easy for the political or religious issues to distract from or overwhelm the main subject of the discourse: the applicant himself. Danish, however, does a good job of using his religious studies and beliefs—very much a central aspect of his identity—to show his dedication to learning, how he self-directs and personalizes his education and how he both learns from and gives back to the people around him whether at home, with communities and groups other than his own or abroad.

Danish shows how important Islam is to him by bookending his essay with key religious quotes. Many applicants start an essay with a quote, and so you run the risk of sounding formulaic, but Danish immediately personalizes the Imam's words by contextualizing them in a singular story showing the start of his intellectual and spiritual journey. The anecdote of the 9-year-old girl's theological question not only directs Danish's path of inquiry and frames the rest of the essay, but also gives him a chance to *show* (not list) qualities about himself: his dedication to religious tolerance and interfaith understanding, his *active* involvement and ability to give serious presentations, his open-mindedness and respect for inquiry and learning no matter the source. By taking the 9-year-old Methodist seriously, Danish shows why we, the readers, should take him seriously as well.

Danish is not afraid to make "big" statements about life, knowledge and religion, showing he's given serious thought to the issues he's exploring, but he also immediately connects those statements to specific examples and steps of his own spiritual and intellectual journey. Not only does he delve deeper into Islam by studying at institutions outside of school, but he also commits to expand his understanding by learning about other religions. On his own he studied Arabic for a better understanding of the scripture, but also reveals how another language can influence a worldview just by its structure. *Implied* throughout his essay is Danish's belief that education and learning are part of daily life and can be found not only in the classroom but in the church, on the streets and everywhere in the community.

Danish concludes his essay showing his dedication to the pursuit of knowledge—a trip to the Holy Mosque of Medina in Arabia—which also concluded and "answered" the religious question posed by the 9-year-old Methodist at the start: in terms of structure the essay, and each supporting paragraph, feels "whole" and complete. Danish, however, uses the ending quote to go beyond the religious to apply it to his character and love of learning as a whole, leaving the reader with a sense that Danish will not only take full advantage of all that the UC has to offer in terms of academics and community, but that he'll also give back and contribute, improving the education of everyone.

## "Lessons from Sojourn"

**Anonymous**
*Accepted by UC Berkeley, UC Irvine and UC Santa Barbara*

FOG OBSCURED THE SAN MATEO SKY, but heat permeated the atmosphere. As Nicole* spewed antagonistic phrases towards Sophia,* the smile slipped from Sophia's fragile face. A tear descended down her now pallid cheek. In our lunch group, no voice rose to defend Sophia, not even my own.

Later, I realized it had been no different from other confrontations: Sophia was teased, and no one defended her. That night, I remembered a similar story that bore a haunting resemblance to this event.

A month before this encounter, I had the unique opportunity to attend Sojourn to the Past, a trip retracing the footsteps that civil rights pioneers paved during the pivotal struggle for justice. During this trip into the bloodstained pages of American history, we met Elizabeth Eckford, one of the Little Rock Nine, whose fight on the frontlines for civil rights left her wounded and scarred, due to taunts from ruthless classmates. Elizabeth's message was simple, her somber words reflective of her repeated mistreatment: "You might be someone's hope someday. You might help someone live another day."

After discerning the parallels between the torment Eckford and Sophia faced, I began my own sojourn, contemplating how I could fix the problems with Sophia. I had been a silent witness, allowing her to fall victim to cruel treatment without defending her. Eckford's story revealed the long-term perils of bullying, and I did not want to be a propagator of similar merciless treatment. I now understood that it was not merely the aggression by Sophia's adversaries that would scar her; it was the silence of her friends, like myself, whose refusal to defend her would hurt her more. No longer could I ignore this injustice. Everyone, including Sophia, deserves to be treated humanely, and have loyal friends who stand up on her behalf.

A few days after this epiphany, Nicole mocked Sophia once again. Instead of ignoring Nicole's diatribe, I stood up for Sophia.

"I am done allowing you to victimize Sophia," I calmly stated, holding Nicole's gaze. "She deserves respect, because she has feelings, too."

Although it has only been six months since learning about the non-violent methods civil rights activists employed to achieve equality and justice, I have carried this newfound determination to defend others into other facets of my life. As a church youth leader, I stress the importance of defending those who are taunted. I have led peaceful conflict resolution and anti-bullying classes for children, hoping to motivate silent witnesses to support the defenseless. Additionally, I have facilitated presentations for teenagers, where I retell Eckford's story, and convey the need to defend those who are abused.

Threading through the halls of school, I exchange a friendly "hello" with Sophia and see a face that no longer bears the scars of a friendless outcast. Determined to heed the lessons I learned from Eckford's story about not being a silent witness, I continue to strive towards guiding others on the path of universal acceptance and compassion.

\* Names have been changed.

## ANALYSIS

"Lessons from Sojourn" shows a high school student putting her learning into action. It is clear that the writer doesn't compartmentalize her education, but rather reflects deeply on what she learns and applies it to her life. She walks us through her thought process as she makes a connection between the Little Rock Nine and her own experiences. She unflinchingly confronts her own past mistakes and then takes bold steps to correct them. While other high schoolers might feel that it's enough not to actively bully others, the writer can recognize that the mere fact of her silence makes her complicit. Her essay is a great example of giving readers an inside look at the process of maturing. She vividly paints two scenes of bullying, creating a before and after picture that shows the impact she has on her peers. Including a direct quote of what she said to confront the bully further makes the scene real for her readers.

Not only does the writer show maturity, but she shows an unusual commitment to acting on her convictions. Few high school students would be brave enough to stand up to a bully, let alone passionate enough to follow-through on their anti-bullying epiphany to lead workshops for children.

The writer provides a unifying thread that shows the underlying motivation between her distinct extracurricular activities. The essay explains that as a church leader, a teacher for children and a workshop presenter, the writer expresses her passion for fighting bullying.

An essay can be a good opportunity to highlight ties between seemingly disparate extracurriculars. Colleges like to see a strong passion rather than a scattershot approach to extracurricular involvement. In this case, the writer is able to make connections not only among separate extracurriculars but also between her personal life, her educational experiences and her activities.

Opening and closing lines are important, and quite noticeable, in a short essay format. The opening of the writer's essay is a bit melodramatic, but it does create enough suspense to draw the reader in. Likewise, although her final line is overstated—"universal acceptance and compassion" is a pretty ambitious goal—her closing is still a forceful restatement of the main thrust of her essay. Keep these basic functions in mind as you write your own opening and closing. An opening should entice the reader to continue, and a closing should be a high-impact statement that does not stray from the essay's main idea.

## "My Greatest Fear"

**Mitchell Brisacher**
*Accepted by UC San Diego and UC Santa Barbara*

*Essay prompt: Personal quality, talent, accomplishment, contribution or experience*

GRAVESTONE UPON GRAVESTONE WITH ROWS AND rows going as far as the eye can see—I was standing right in the middle of the vast expanse confronting "My Greatest Fear." The result was a sextych and a Silver Key.

Although it sounds like the plot to *National Treasure,* where I would have to obtain the silver key to unlock Thomas Jefferson's secret diary, in actuality, it was an opportunity to conquer my greatest fear through my greatest passion. The prompt said to photograph my "greatest unease in life, while still revealing tangible and relatable elements of the outer being." I could see everyone in the class grimace slightly as they felt the two-ton ball of nerves and anxiety gather in their stomachs as they thought about their special person, place or idea that personally filled them with terror. I was no exception.

Death: horrible, vile and cold. To capture death's true essence, I took the short car drive to The Los Angeles National Cemetery, while trying to shake off the feeling of dread over the entire trip there. Chills tickled my spine as I pulled into the parking lot. I turned off the car and slowly opened my door. It was a bright and sunny day, but to me it felt like a moonless night on Friday the thirteenth because that's the sense of doom that fell over me. The sun reflected off the marble white gravestones, creating illusion that they went on forever, trapping me in the middle of never-ending death.

I jumped right into the ocean of death and fully submerged myself in the fear. I shot the photo project with a friend and a tripod and used self-portraiture to embrace my fear. I got up close and personal to convey my view of the bleakness of death. Self-portraiture allows an honest and convincing representation of self, and I was able to immerse myself through it.

After the photo shoot, I spent hours poring over the chill-inducing images, trying to communicate the sense of horror that emerged within me. Using Photoshop as my chosen medium, I enhanced the pictures to amplify their power. Tons of photographs ended up on the cutting room floor as I searched for the perfect image. Pictures I thought were perfect just could not capture the feeling that overwhelmed me every time death was encountered. In the end, I created sextych, a series of six pictures that work together to increase the strength and power of the image as a whole.

The result of my internal struggle to overcome the fear of death was The Scholastic Art & Writing Awards of 2011 Silver Key for Excellence in Visual Arts. The announcement was made at a school assembly, and I swelled with pride as my photograph was shown on the big screen. I had conquered my adversary, and in the process, I produced my best photographs to date. The recognition that the Award provided proved to me that I could overcome my greatest fear while exploring what I loved. Thanks to my greatest passion my greatest fear, death, no longer fills the pit of my gut with cement.

### ANALYSIS

Mitchell opens this essay with a quirky first line that sounds more sci-fi than common app. Once he has captured the reader's attention, Mitchell explains the premise of the essay and describes a challenge he was presented with: "to photograph [his] 'greatest unease in life, while still revealing tangible and relatable elements of the outer being.'" By using the photography assignment as a frame for the piece, Mitchell sets up a clear narrative arc, from receiving an intimidating assignment, to attacking it, to mastering it.

In the body of the essay, Mitchell vividly conjures up a sense of his fear and dread at confronting death in the Los Angeles National Cemetery, using sensory details like "sun reflected off the marble white gravestones" to set the scene. Mitchell's description of the photographic techniques he employed shows his mastery of the terms and tools of the art form. For instance, he builds credibility when he writes, "Self-portraiture allows an honest and convincing representation of self," and when he describes his decision to create a sextych, a "series of six pictures that work together to increase the strength and power of the image as a whole."

The reader experiences Mitchell's artistic process along with him, from the chilling car ride to the cemetery all the way through the hours spent modifying the images using Photoshop. By giving the reader a window into his painstaking work, Mitchell communicates his dedication to his project and his ability to stick with it until he achieves the best possible result.

Mitchell focuses on the personal growth and internal sense of satisfaction that came along with winning an award, rather than on the external praise he garnered. Rather than simply being proud to be recognized, he is proud to have successfully used photography to deal with one of his greatest fears. Although it is perhaps a stretch to believe that Mitchell is completely free of his fear of death thanks to this one project, it is nonetheless clear that he has developed a sophisticated understanding of art's cathartic power.

This is a good example of an essay that expands upon an accomplishment that may be listed elsewhere in the application but not necessarily given much weight. An admissions officer might read that Mitchell won the Silver Key for Excellence in Visual Arts and quickly forget that fact, especially if his or her brain is full of information about other applicants who have also won art awards. Thanks to the essay, however, Mitchell can flesh out the true meaning of this accomplishment and show not only his technical skill as a photographer but also his capacity for self-reflection as an artist.

## "A Brutal Blemish"

**Brian Tashjian**
*Accepted by UC Berkeley, UCLA and UC San Diego*

I COULD NOT FACE MYSELF IN the mirror. What used to be a few blemishes on a relatively smooth face had turned into numerous large, painful, red swellings—too many to count. One of them, the Everest of this infectious mountain range, had grown to be close to the size of an eyeball. Two eyes were enough for me, but Mother Nature had different plans while I spent my six weeks in Central America, with only bacteria-infected water to wash my face. Although it only took a month to develop, the physical and emotional consequences that accompanied this breakout of severe acne lasted almost a year. It was the stares, the double-takes, the looks away, even one very blunt person commenting, "Wow, you have really bad acne."

I knew they were not purposefully trying to react, but I saw their expression change nonetheless. But more than the reactions from others, what crushed me the most were my own reactions. I could not look anyone in the eye, afraid of what they might see. I could not look at myself and every time I washed my face, I was reminded that it was more than just visually unpleasant; there was topography. However, despite the uphill self-esteem battle, pushing through what I had to face (literally) helped more than it hurt emotionally. I learned a lot about myself and others during that year. My real best friends showed themselves by supporting me through before, during, and after. I learned that even though something may last longer than expected, and even though something may reoccur more than I feel is needed, I have the strength to remain who I am throughout that struggle. Luckily though, the struggle ended with the introduction of a powerful drug, and the light at the end of the tunnel was a bright one. Without that year-long period, I would not be who I am today; I would not know myself as well as I do. And I definitely would not be as confident going forward in life as I am right now.

### ANALYSIS

This essay accomplishes the basic task of an essay on a personal challenge: communicating how that challenge has helped the writer grow. Brian communicates what he suffered, but changes direction partway through the essay to talk about what he learned from it. He begins with a hook that begs the question, "Why?" and encourages the reader to read on. From there, he gives a painfully descriptive account of the acne outbreak he suffered. The descriptions are creative—"there was topography"—and even show a sense of humor about a very difficult situation—"Two eyes were enough for me, but Mother Nature had different plans." He also recounts the reactions he had to face from other people, giving the reader a sense of the emotional as well as physical consequences of his problem. Perhaps the most telling observation in the essay is Brian's blunt description of his *own* reaction to his problem. He is not afraid to confess that the outbreak dealt a harsh blow to his self-esteem and ability to interact confidently with his peers. Because he candidly admits how deeply affected he was by the situation, his ability to learn from it is all the more impressive.

At the end of his essay, Brian shows that he had the maturity to endure and even grow from this experience. He learned who his real friends were, found unknown reserves of personal strength and became more confident. Readers can tell from his philosophical take on the incident that he has the maturity to see the good and the opportunities for growth involved in a challenging circumstance.

If you are contemplating how to write about a challenge in your own life, Brian's three-stage model might work for you: describe the problem, outline its implications (especially its effect upon you internally) and then, most importantly, elucidate what you learned from it. Evocative descriptions like Brian's, especially if they reveal maturity and a sense of humor, will be important in the "exposition" section of the essay in which you explain the problem to the reader. Diving into a dramatic aspect of the problem with a creative hook will foster curiosity. Vivid descriptions of the issue make for good opening sections. Once you have established the situation at a basic level and made clear why it was a problem, you can delve more deeply into its psychological and social impacts. In the case of this essay, you could think about the first section as describing what happened to the author's face and the second section as describing what happened to his psyche as a result. Finally, and most importantly, offer some sense of the self-realizations that came out of the situation. This is not to say that you have to turn any negative situation into a positive one, but that your essay should build up to a revelation not just of struggle but ultimately of strength.

# 14

# TALENT

## "Convincing"

**Inès C. Gérard-Ursin**
*Accepted by all of the UC schools*

*Essay prompt: Personal quality, talent, accomplishment, contribution or experience*

I CAN CONVINCE PEOPLE.

I do admit it is not an extraordinary, exceptionally tough skill to acquire: yet I'm good at it. If I have learned anything from the cultures I have touched, it is this special power, the ability to perceive and adapt psychological and social codes in order to achieve a specific aim.

I was not even fully aware of this until one sweltering afternoon, after several nights of minimal sleep and cafeteria meals, I found myself locked in the basement of the Arlington Sheraton armed with two pretend legislative wing men, a resolution, and a disarming smile. The three of us represented the Russia group at the Global Young Leaders Conference held in Washington D.C. and New York during the height of summer: although the purpose of the conference was largely to connect young people from different parts of the world, this afternoon our focus was on solving the border crisis in Cyprus. We were 45 teenagers in one debate room, all with our own opinions and our own resolutions. As the Faculty Advisors set time off for negotiations, our secretary drew a deep shaky breath: "Let's do this."

In 20 minutes I had managed to convince ten countries to sign our resolution, and we were moving into voting procedure. I was still filled with that rush, the after effect of single minded, straightforward persuasion, and my limbs were tingling, my heart was racing.

Yet our one opponent, the UK, had a similarly determined disposition; facing the failure of her own resolution, she vetoed ours. Even still, my greatest sense of accomplishment came when the room erupted in passionate cries and accusations: I sat back, satisfied, and enjoyed it. The Faculty Advisors had to send us to dinner; the "formal debate" was going nowhere. Later, in meeting with our complete Russia group, we were proud to confirm that we were the only delegation that had won a debate, if only "in our hearts."

Ever since, I have become more aware of my love of persuasion, of diplomatic discussion and quick improvisation. Reading people is my skill. Although moving seven times, extensive travelling, being a member of a multicultural family, and attending an International School has strengthened and helped me develop it, I still like to take at least partial responsibility for the level of my ability today. In my youth I had to figure out the social codes of three countries quickly, and then adapt in order to survive. Now I am just a convincing teenage girl who knows what she's talking about.

I am a dangerous person.

The question is, have I convinced you?

## ANALYSIS

Inès bookends her essay with short, declarative sentences: "I can convince people" and "I am a dangerous person." It's a good strategy for her, since it underscores her ability to get her audience's attention and to boldly make a point—part of what makes her a persuasive person. The essay has style and even sass. Just after Inès gives a litany of experiences that sharpened her ability to read people, veering closer to classic college essay tropes, she firmly asserts her own voice and attitude: "Now I am just a convincing teenage girl who knows what she's talking about." She doesn't sound like a textbook example of the ideal college applicant. She sounds like *herself*—an opinionated, outspoken young woman with a strong sense of who she is and what she can do. Writing a college essay is not about doing your best impression of the perfect student. The only voice you can successfully write in is your own, and that's hard enough.

This piece is an example of using a vignette to support an argument. Persuasive essays don't need to be formulaic essay-test style compilations of dry examples that all drive home a single point. As Inès clearly knows, stories can be powerful ways to convince people. The bulk of her essay is a well-evoked scene at a Global Young Leaders Conference. Since she has successfully employed declarative statements in her opening to outline her main points, she does not need to explicitly drive them home while narrating her story. Instead, she uses longer, more detailed and more dramatic sentences to spin a tale that illustrates her love of argument. The story uses details to create an emotional impact. The readers can feel the nervousness imbued in the secretary's "deep shaky breath" and sense Inès' post-debate exhilaration through her description of her tingling limbs and racing heart.

Perhaps the boldest part of the essay is the closing line. Ending with a rhetorical question is a risky move. The point of a well-placed rhetorical question is to reach out from the paper and engage directly with your audience. In the hands of unskilled writers, however, rhetorical questions can feel like shortcuts to making an impact. Use them with caution. In this case, the question fits the essay's sassy tone as well as its content. Inès shows that she's a well-practiced persuader able to use a variety of rhetorical devices.

## "Cross Country"

**Anonymous**
*Accepted by UC Berkeley, UC Davis, UCLA, UC San Diego and UC Santa Cruz*

*Essay prompt: Personal quality, talent, accomplishment, contribution or experience*

I AM THE CAPTAIN OF A strange pack of misunderstood athletes: long-distance runners. We hear phrases like, "anyone can run—that's not a sport." Oh it is a sport—just not a sport for the weak or the weak-minded. Long distance running requires an immense amount of endurance, both physical and mental, because after three miles of thinking, "this hurts," it's very difficult to motivate yourself to run another three. Before high school, I had never done anything athletic. I was a perpetual whiner. By all counts, cross country was not the sport for me. And after the first day of practice my freshman year, I almost quit. But I had made a commitment, and I was going to stick to it. So I kept coming to practice; even after weeks of dreading the end of the school day; even after we had our first practice in the rain, a day so miserable that the drops mixed in with the tears rolling down my face; even after I got shin splints, that oh-so-common runner's injury that makes running feel akin to hobbling on two wooden pegs; even then I stuck it out.

And so I got stronger. My body got used to running for an hour without stopping; my mind got used to the pain. Practice stopped being absolute torture and started being what it should have been—a workout. And suddenly, after two months, my hard work paid off, and I did the unthinkable—I started winning! No longer was running something I just did. It was something that showcased what I could do, what I was truly capable of. As I improved, so did the team, and suddenly I had twice the motivation—I wasn't just running for personal gain, I wasn't just running for me. I was running because my team, the girls who had suffered along with me on those awful days, the ones who understood the pain and hardship that came with running, the ones cheering for me as I crossed the finish line, needed me.

This is my fourth year as a member of the Cross Country team and my third as a Varsity member. These past seasons have been full of hardships, failures, and breakdowns. But I have also had my share of successes, victories, and moments of pure jubilation. Looking back, I would say that deciding to stay in cross country was one of the most significant decisions I have made in my life, because this sport has molded me into the person I am today. I have learned how to persevere, and I have seen the tangible results of my hard work. I have learned how to persist through pain, how to acknowledge it and then push past it. I have learned how to put aside everything for the good of my team, and how this team becomes a family. And from this family I have learned leadership: how to inspire, encourage, support and provide direction.

## ANALYSIS

Every year college and university admissions officers read *hundreds* of essays that follow this pattern:

> ➤ I tried out for a sport

> ➤ I was not good

> ➤ I hurt a lot

> ➤ I stuck at it

> ➤ I got better

> ➤ I started seeing (especially after one "ah-hah!" moment) the sport as an important part of me

> ➤ The sport has taught me dedication, leadership, teamwork, perseverance, etc.

Creative writers can disguise the formulistic aspects of the "sports essay" with sensory details *showing* us the world instead of just telling us about it, and then go beyond it by connecting the sport to many other topics of interest and experiences that flesh out a well-rounded portrait of the writer (see Jackie Botts' "Dance" essay on page 150). Struggling writers follow the "script" listed above.

While it's totally okay to follow the pattern—it is, after all, a progression of events and emotions that many athletes have gone through—at least use it, as the writer of "Cross Country" did, as an opportunity to demonstrate your writing competence as well as show a side of you beyond just the athlete.

The writer immediately defines her sport not only as a physically challenging activity, but as one that requires mental toughness as well. She gives us a portrait of herself before cross country: a whiney couch potato. But we also get a glimpse of some of her core values: "I made a commitment, and I was going to stick to it." (Understandably, universities want students who will finish their degrees). And we see for ourselves that she can write well and *show* with sensory details: " . . . even after we had our first practice in the rain, a day so miserable that the drops mixed in with the tears rolling down my face . . . ".

The writer then expands the spotlight of the essay to include, not just herself, but her team as well: " . . . suddenly I had twice the motivation—I wasn't just running for personal gain, I wasn't just running for me." Universities love to see that applicants value the team / group / community as well as themselves, as the whole point of attending a university is to actively participate in a community of scholars, athletes and activists, not only during your years of coursework but for the rest of your life: people take great pride in saying "I'm a Bruin" or "I'm a Banana Slug" just as much as the universities themselves like to boast of their famous alumni.

In her last paragraph the writer spells out the lessons learned. She saves the section from sounding formulaic by using more descriptive diction ("jubilation") as well as artful use of alliteration: "I have learned how to persist through pain, how to acknowledge it and then push past it." She shows that she will be a success in the classroom as well as on the cross country course.

## "Stepping onto the Stage"

**Amber Fearon**
*Accepted by UC Berkeley, UC Davis, UC Irvine, UCLA, UC Santa Cruz and UC San Diego*

MY HEART WAS BEATING SO FAST it felt as though it was going to burst out of my chest. I could feel my hands becoming clammy and sweat collecting on my forehead. A week earlier one of my friends had asked me if I'd like to sing with his band, CrisP, in our high school 'Battle of the Bands'. I jumped at the opportunity, forgetting my stage fright and insecurities about my singing abilities. Now all of a sudden I found myself holding a 'mike' center stage. I looked across the grassy field to see my fellow classmates, teachers, and parents waiting for us to start. Gripping the microphone tightly, I began to sway to the beat of "Coastin'" by Zion I. The first piano chords drifted into the audience and the beat of the drums matched the rhythm of my heart. I looked over at my fellow singer, Nicole, for reassurance, but all I saw was confusion. She tapped her microphone, but there was no sound. The chorus was quickly approaching, and all of a sudden I was facing a solo, instead of the rehearsed duet. I took a deep breath to steady myself. I shut my eyes for a second, and went for it. As the song ended, I glanced into the crowd of staring faces; there was dead silence. My heart tightened at the thought of failure, but then the crowd erupted into cheers. With relief, a huge grin spread across my face—I had done it! In a flash the ballots were tallied and I joined my band members, as we crossed our fingers in anticipation of the announcement. Our band's name was called! We had taken first place and our week of intense practice had paid off.

I was overjoyed by our win, until I heard that our prize was the chance to perform in front of the entire school. My heart dropped once again, but this time I had the experience and confidence to stand in front of my classmates and sing out. I knew what I could do if I challenged myself. After singing in front of the school, I realized the truth in this quote: *"To laugh is to risk appearing the fool...To place your ideas, your dreams before the crowd, is to risk their loss . . . To live is to risk dying...To try is to risk failure. But risks must be taken; because the greatest hazard in life is to risk nothing" -Anonymous.*

While I've had confidence in areas such as running for captain of my soccer team, maintaining good grades and welcoming new students to campus through New Crew, I've always been shy in choir. Instead of auditioning for a solo or the lead role in the school musical, I've volunteered to work behind the scenes. However, after revealing a different side of myself at Battle of the Bands, I gained self-confidence and pride in my musical abilities and learned the benefits of taking risks. Now I want to challenge myself further with solos in choir, memberships in new clubs and different events track and field events. I've always realized that through hard work I can achieve my goals, but singing in Battle of the Bands has taken that understanding to a new level. This newfound confidence has made me see the world in a new light, and realize that opportunities are open to me if I try.

## ANALYSIS

Amber begins in the middle of her anecdote, letting her reader feel almost as alienated as she does as she says, "My heart was beating so fast it felt as though it was going to burst out of my chest. I could feel my hands becoming clammy and sweat collecting on my forehead." Details, from the sweat on her forehead to the name of the song and the band, add to the scene's vividness. Her style is peppered with short sentences that build on each other: "I jumped at the opportunity, forgetting my stage fright and insecurities about my singing abilities. Now all of a sudden I found myself holding a 'mike' center stage," for example, or "The chorus was quickly approaching, and all of a sudden I was facing a solo, instead of the rehearsed duet. I took a deep breath to steady myself. I shut my eyes for a second, and went for it. As the song ended, I glanced into the crowd of staring faces; there was dead silence." This cadence propels the reader inexorably towards the chorus, the end of the song and even the band's win.

But Amber's essay isn't just showcasing her style and artistic writing, nor is it a self-aggrandizing account of how great her band was. She surprises us by telling us "I was overjoyed by our win" and then saying, "until I heard that our prize was the chance to perform in front of the entire school." Amber's admission of shyness and nervousness is particularly striking not only in light of her huge success that she has just related, but also because it is makes the preceding anecdote all the more poignant. Amber makes the readers understand just how high the stakes were for her, and just how transformative her success was.

Amber may be doing herself a disservice by, rather than describing this transformation in her own words, using the quote to do it for her. But she has very clearly demonstrated the dramatic risk she took in front of the crowd, and, with her effusive style in describing her band's win, she clearly communicates that the joy and self-confidence she derives from having taken that risk far outweighs her fears.

The honesty and vividness with which Amber portrays her fears allows her to fill this essay with her successes in music, in sports and in school without sounding too self-aggrandizing and without being off-putting; Amber is clearly reflecting on a major concern in her life, rather than contriving a weakness in order to sound more modest. Her focus on a single event and anecdote, too, makes it clear how extensive her fear was and how important overcoming it was. Finally, she ends on an encouraging and uplifting note but avoids sounding too canned by including specifics: "Now I want to challenge myself further with solos in choir, memberships in new clubs and different track and field events." Amber avoids making extravagant claims and sticks to the specifics, which in fact heightens the personal nature of her essay and brings her very vividly to life in the mind of the reader.

## "Dance"

**Jackie Botts**
*Accepted by UC Berkeley, UCLA and UC Santa Barbara*

*Essay prompt: Describe the world you come from and how your world has shaped you*

I WAS FOUR WHEN I TOOK my first dance class. At eight, I discovered ballet was more than pliés and tutus. As my teacher played a sweet melody, I began to dart around the room like a hummingbird I had seen in our garden. For the first time I realized that through movement, I could represent ideas and express emotions. I was just beginning to fall in love with ballet, unaware that the world of dance—its intense classes and euphoric performances, the purpose and awareness of a step thoughtfully executed—would come to define my own world.

By freshman year I was consumed. When asked what I wanted to be, I relished the surprised expressions at my response: a ballerina. A friend asked if a student as focused as I shouldn't dedicate her life to something more academic—wouldn't I prefer thinking to moving?

I was learning, however, that thought is what elevates movement into an art form. In English class, I read *Siddhartha,* who taught me to walk more slowly and breathe more deeply. Siddhartha lived so purposefully; he would spend hours by a river, eliminating external distractions as he turned his mind inward. In ballet class, I stopped relying only on the mirror, instead tuning my mind to my body. *How would Siddhartha dance?* was a slightly comic yet fascinating question. Meanwhile, in physical therapy for several injuries, I realized that I could no longer "just dance through the pain," but that a dancer must be intelligent about her body. Like Siddhartha, she must be aware and move with purpose.

A year later, as I prepared for the Biology Subject Test, the concept of awareness took on a more complex meaning. With my hefty prep book propped up on my stomach, rising and falling with my breath, I read about the alveoli in my lungs and about my stalwart heart, which relentlessly propels blood cells and oxygen through every part of my body. Like many dancers, I had often pushed my body beyond its limits, ignoring its signals as I strove for unattainable perfection. Biology taught me that I must not separate my mind from my body; the two must work in tandem.

These ideas converged when I read Annie Dillard in junior year English. Dillard writes, "Today...you know you're alive. You take huge steps, trying to feel the planet's roundness arc between your feet." What awareness, what purposefulness one would need to sense the curvature of the earth as one walked! What if I could dance like that? What if I could know my body with such wakefulness; aware of every muscular function, of the biological processes fueling each movement? And what if I could define the concept behind each step I executed so deliberately that others would experience the dance as acutely as I do?

Then, I think, I might be a true artist.

Over the past few years, several injuries have led me to give up my dream of becoming a professional ballerina, yet dance remains my passion and the lens through which I view the world. Regardless of what I study or what career I pursue, I will approach each challenge ahead of me as I would any dance—with intention and dedication, mindful of each step. I will endeavor to feel the curve of the Earth beneath my feet and I will strive to encounter others with clarity and honesty. When I dance, I am aware and charged with purpose, and that is how I intend to live.

## ANALYSIS

Eyes travel like fleeting feet over Jackie's essay as we slip on her shoes and follow her steps as she discovers dance, links it to literature and then absorbs it into her present and future self. By using her dance experience and development as her central conceit (main idea), Jackie provides her essay with a strong framework that allows her to flow effortlessly from step to step, from topic to topic, and to connect her various interests and evolving worldview within a cohesive and "complete" composition. Remember that application readers pour over *hundreds* of essays, many poorly or formulaically written, and so presenting a well-crafted portrait that's easy to read singles you out and casts a bright, positive light on you. Jackie's essay, with its tightly-woven structure, sentences that flow in a graceful rhythm of short and long and astute personal reflection, is, at the very *least*, a joy to read.

Each paragraph clearly advances a new idea, aspect or evolution while seamlessly flowing from the previous and on through the following. Jackie's intro is also her introduction to dance, and we feel her child-like joy as well as her adult apprehension as she foreshadows how overpowering a part dance would become later in her life. The reader also, at this point, gets worried that this will be another "Sports taught me dedication and perseverance" essay that focuses more on the sport / activity than the applicant.

Notice, however, how Jackie uses her friend in the second paragraph to set up the *real* thesis of her essay: "I was learning . . . that thought is what elevates movement into an art form." She then spends the next three paragraphs showing her evolving worldview by giving concrete examples of how she applied other studies to her understanding of both her dance and herself. Reading *Siddhartha* led to inward reflection (cleverly contraposed with the symbol of the dance studio mirror that showed only the physical appearance) and thus awareness of self. The biology textbook, both its content and physical mass, gave Jackie a better understanding of her body and how to be mindful of seeing the corporal and cerebral as a whole. And reading Dillard expanded her focus beyond the horizon—a literal worldview—to come to an understanding of art and life as empathy.

Jackie ends her essay by tying all the earlier threads together to present a complete portrait of herself, using strong declarations of her matured identity and applying all that is "dance" to all other aspects of her life. Admissions officers, in addition to being pleased at reading well-written and well-structured essays that flow, love to see how an applicant has reflected on personal experiences, how those experiences contribute to the person she is today and how she will use them to face the challenges ahead. "Aware and charged with purpose" is a great last phrase to leave in the reader's mind and connected to your name.

## "Just One More"

**Jaimie Copprell**
*Accepted by UC Berkeley, UC Davis, UC Irvine, UCLA, UC Riverside, UC San Diego, UC Santa Barbara and UC Santa Cruz*

*Essay prompt: Personal quality, talent, accomplishment, contribution or experience*

IT WAS A LOVE-HATE RELATIONSHIP. MY heart struggled at times to maintain the pace, but I nonetheless thrived from the strength it gave me each day. For the past three years, my involvement in Cross Country has allowed me to test my endurance, and on numerous levels, to dig deep for reservoirs of strength I never knew I possessed. Most people do not find running miles on end to be very appealing, but to me, it is a revitalizing pastime I am proud to call my own.

Preparation for races and daily practices were often exhausting and at times disappointing, but despite such difficulties, it was the feeling of overcoming adversity that I loved the most. For reasons beyond my control, I have experienced three significant changes in my coach each year; I had to adjust to new techniques, expectations, and coaching methods. Though I knew it would take some getting used to, it was a challenge I was willing to face. Adapting to this change ensures me that I am capable of withstanding any unexpected obstacle life may throw at me.

Aside from overcoming these changes, I anticipated the races the most. To me, racing was not about defeating my opponents, but rather an opportunity to test my will to succeed under unimaginably difficult conditions. This created an inner-drive that motivated me to do my best in the classroom, at home, and most importantly, as a person. And in racing, it all came down to myself and what amount of pain I was willing to endure and still be able to walk away knowing I gave it my all. Whether I ran the race of my life or suffered an unexpected defeat, I could always count on my team to support me. In these three years, I have had the privilege of having a very supportive "second" family. And to this day, I still thrive on the motivation my teammates have given me and the lessons my coaches have bestowed on me.

My very first coach once told me that in races, "Think of it as being your last—your only—and all you need is just one more." I never got to asking him what he meant by "just one more," but I perceive it as being a reason to not give up. I have just one more mile, one more step, one more chance to seize everything I ever wanted. Whether I nailed his interpretation correctly or not, I do not plan on changing my own. This is who I have become and in my life, I am in a race to succeed—to reap every learning opportunity available. And I am stopping for no one.

## ANALYSIS

Jaimie uses her involvement with cross country in order to discuss how she is able to overcome challenges. In the UC experience essay, it is important for students to show not only what they've accomplished, but also what challenges they faced and how they dealt with these challenges. Jaimie successfully does this by discussing the physical and mental challenges she faced while on her school's cross country team.

First of all, Jaimie notes that physically, cross country tested her endurance and physical strength. This is commendable, but it's also true for most high school athletes involved in competition. Therefore, instead of spending time talking about being physically tested, Jaimie turns the focus towards her unique experience. Jaimie had to adapt to three different coaches over the course of her high school career. On the surface, having three coaches doesn't seem like a particularly important detail. Yet, Jackie notes that the changes in coaching staff also meant adapting to "new techniques, expectations, and coaching methods." In this way, Jaimie illustrates the unique challenges she faced, communicating to the audience the types of adversity she is capable of overcoming. Still, Jaimie could have taken some time to explain specifically how she adapted to the changes the coaches made her make. This would have given us a greater understanding of how Jaimie uses her own skills to adapt to novel circumstances.

Similarly, Jaimie notes that she overcame "unimaginably difficult conditions" while racing. Again, Jaimie's ability to overcome these challenges is impressive, yet there are no specifics to what "unimaginably difficult conditions" means. Was it physical pain, mental conditions, weather? Specifying the conditions she faced would have given the reader a clearer picture of the range of difficulties Jaimie was able to overcome.

It's important that Jaimie is specific about what she is capable of, because she relates her ability to overcome obstacles in cross country to her ability to face difficulties in other aspects of her life. If Jaimie is specific about what mental barriers she can surpass during racing, then we can predict the sort of psychological challenges she might be able to overcome at school. We can see the effectiveness of this tactic when Jaimie describes her admirable personal qualities. For example, Jaimie talks about finding satisfaction in a race even when defeated. This shows humility. Likewise, Jaimie's acknowledgement of her team's support illustrates her ability to fit into a community and thrive in an environment where she must work with others.

The final paragraph at last gives the reader insight into Jaimie's thought process. We see Jaimie take the words of her coach and give them her own meaning. This shows that Jaimie is attentive, looking for ways to become inspired. This interpretation informs us what Jaimie aspires to do. She encourages herself to grab every opportunity she can, pushing through every last step as if it's the last one she can take to succeed. Jaimie thus proves that she will actively take advantage of all the opportunities that college may have to offer her.

# 15

# TRAVEL

## "Defining Moments"

**Shelby Newallis**
*Accepted by UC San Diego and UC Santa Barbara*

*Essay prompt: Personal quality, talent, accomplishment, contribution or experience*

PEERING OUT OF THE SHUT WINDOW of an overcrowded bus, veering towards the edge of the cliff, I honestly feared for my life. Previously, I had never thought about my last moments, and as I reflected about various people and experiences, I found myself praying, "Please God, I'm not ready yet. I'm sorry that I don't pray often, just not yet, not now." It was during that treacherous excursion along the winding roads of the Italian coastline that I pondered the relevance of my existence: Who am I really? What has my life been truly about? Has my life actually been fulfilling?

Though it may sound like a cliché, my life *has* changed from that day. No, I did not go through a complete transformation in the forty-five minutes from Salerno to Atrani, but this potentially fatal incident catalyzed an internal cultural renaissance. I have had some time to think about what motivates, excites, and inspires me. Coming to the realization of my strong ties to my Italian heritage, specifically the language and culture, I will continue to study Italian and strive to master this romance language and rich culture so that I may share this passion with others. Studying and speaking Italian satisfies my true love for learning and experiencing, which is insatiable.

Life experiences help to define a person and as I enter adulthood, this realization is very apparent. Traveling abroad and meeting new people have taught me that all people possess innate qualities that positively affect others. Sitting with a couple of friends playing cards on the patio of our hotel in Sicily, I saw Salvatore, our bus driver on the tour. He was standing against the wall smoking a cigarette looking over at us as we were laughing and playing cards. Obviously, the language barrier excluded this seemingly interesting man from joining us. After impulsively inviting him to sit with us, I taught him how to play Speed, an American card game. At all times he waited patiently while I tried to communicate in Italian. From this experience I learned a valuable life lesson: we all need to recognize and appreciate the gifts of others, while remembering to reciprocate by sharing our gifts. While I discovered Salvatore's gift of patience, I quickly discovered my own too, that of making others feel comfortable and welcome.

I have been so fortunate to live a life full of memorable experiences by traveling, spending time with family, and meeting new people, like Salvatore. These past experiences have now only intensified my thirst for learning new languages, discovering new cultures, and more importantly being able to experience the uniqueness that all people have to offer.

## ANALYSIS

A near-death experience is one way to start your essay with a bang. In "Defining Moments," Shelby makes a great connection between the content of her essay and its setting. It's fitting that her moment of soul-searching on a lurching bus took place in Italy, because the result of her soul-searching is the realization that she is passionate about Italian culture. Shelby coins a memorable, pitch perfect phrase, "internal cultural renaissance," to describe her epiphanies.

Some other aspects of Shelby's second paragraph should be examined. If, in an essay, you find yourself writing, "Though it may sound like a cliché," odds are that it *is* a cliché and you should avoid it. Statements like, "my true love for learning and experiencing, which is insatiable" are more general. After all, most applicants to a good college probably have a passion for "learning and experiencing."

The essay picks up steam again when Shelby relates another vivid anecdote, this time about an external interaction as well as an internal realization. She reveals her uniquely welcoming instincts by relating how she reached out to her Italian bus driver. Not only that, but she acknowledges with grace and humility that the credit for this positive interaction goes as much to the driver as to her. The story is a great choice for a college essay, because it allows her winning personality and kind heart to shine through. It also gives a concrete example of why she loves learning Italian and the types of positive experiences that language and cultural fluency make possible.

Shelby manages to communicate both her academic passions and her personal qualities, all while keeping the essay tight by centering it on a trip to Italy. In brainstorming ideas for your own essays, consider listing moments in your life in which you demonstrated your best self. Like Shelby's card game, they can be small moments. The important thing is that they show something about who you are that differentiates you from the pack. It's an added plus if you can relate that unique quality to your academic interests or what you can add to a campus.

# 16

# VIGNETTE

**"The World of Bus Stops"**

**Inès C. Gérard-Ursin**
*Accepted by all of the UC schools*

*Essay prompt: Describe the world you come from and how your world has shaped you*

MY WORLD IS THE WORLD OF bus stops. Early mornings, long afternoons spent dreaming, watching the sun's rays warm the spots of dew through enchanted mist. I dream of transcribing every scene into my journal, of making time stop so I can breathe in the landscape and cement the feeling of wonder in my being. I live for those quiet moments of beauty at bus stops.

At one of the last assemblies before the summer break, I remember a student comparing our school to a train station, with people forever coming and going, or stopping to stare into space for a little while. Sometimes I speculate whether the comfort I find from buses are from their lack of permanence, the fact that they are not in one set position, but going from one place to another, and that I can just relax in this state of transience. I am moving on to something better, and am happy with exactly where I am.

It was not always so: long ago in my first year facing a new public transport system, I managed to extend a 20 minute ride home to four hours. Taking three buses, a tram, and finally a taxi in the Norwegian winter darkness, I stumbled through the front door exhausted, having used up all my money on payphones and having spent all my energy staggering around in huge ski boots. Similarly, the first time we moved to Norway I spent weeks stumbling through idioms and childish rhymes, but as I have grown to learn how to use the public transportation system, so have I learned to slide back in to Norwegian culture, and I feel like a fully integrated Norwegian-American-Belgian member of society. In the period of social adjustment, all is doubt and experimentation, but once I figure things out I am ready to set off and pursue my ambitions.

But, right now, the bus windows are so dirty they close us off from the outside, they make the world inside an isolated gold orb, filled with platinum blonde hair buns, small heart tattoos, baseball caps and baby carriages. Everything besides the here and now ceases to exist, life stops for a moment and my dreams duplicate and mutate to fill every empty seat. The clear voice of a British political commentator, jangling through my headphones, fills the air and drowns out all distractions with its righteousness, and I glance up through tales of Republican nominees to catch a brief glimpse of clear blue, rose-rimmed sky.

Is it weird to feel that I am flying?

On bus rides I gather hope, I harness ideas, vitality, energy, for the moments when I step off. Staring out the windows of this metal beast, I have realized some of my greatest hopes. I wish to speak for those who cannot, to use all that I can to accomplish good in the world, I wish to have a direct say in political legislation, and I wish to help others see beauty, see happiness, in the own mundane elements of their lives. I would like to save someone with my words.

Life is a dream until we pull up into the station, and I put away my headphones and glimpse a friend through the dirt-crusted windows. Then, it is time to make all my wishes come true.

## ANALYSIS

Inès starts off with a simple yet resounding opener that states a direct answer to the prompt. From the outset, she combines vivid imagery about her experience on buses with profound reflections expressed in phrases such as, "sometimes I speculate whether the comfort I find from buses are from their lack of permanence" and "I am moving on to something better, and am happy with exactly where I am."

The essay isn't all poetic evocation and philosophical musing, however. Inès also disarms the reader with a humorous peek into her first stumbling Norwegian bus ride. She shows that she is capable of writing at a high level and of analyzing her life deeply but also includes this humanizing vignette. The details of the story that she provides help readers identify with her and her predicament. It's hard not to feel sympathy for her when you picture her wearily trudging around an unfamiliar place in her "huge ski boots." The purpose of the story isn't to seek pity, but rather to show how far she has come and to underscore her ability to adjust to new situations.

Inès cleverly segues between buses and her career interests by mentioning the political commentary she listens to on her rides. It becomes clear in her final paragraphs that she is interested in politics and that she has identified her own facility with words. Yet she is smart not to commit herself to any particular career too definitively. It isn't necessary to give exhaustive specifics about your future plans in a college essay. Since many students change their minds over the course of their four years in college, it can even be counterproductive to come across as dead-set on a single path. Sounding too decided can come across as naive or even disingenuous. You don't want to give the impression that you have prematurely narrowed your interests or, worse yet, to seem as if you are merely telling admissions officers what you think they want to hear. Some students may be tempted to avow a definite commitment to a particular career path out of a fear of sounding aimless or indecisive. By contrast, Inès shows that she has put careful thought into what she cares about and what skills she has to offer, but avoids painting herself into a corner by over-committing to a defined plan.

# 17

# ADVICE ON TOPICS FROM UNIVERSITY OF CALIFORNIA STUDENTS

### Showing Who I Am

"For my admission essay, I chose something that showed who I was to the core. I knew I had to write about something that showed why I was remarkable and the only way I knew how to do that was by picking a topic that resembled the person I was, am and desired to be. Thus, I wrote about how I cared for my elderly grandparents. It showed how I overcame hardships, it touched upon my best qualities and how I wanted to continue to help others."

—*Catherine Bronzo, UCLA*

### A Different Kind of Challenge

"One of the topics I was asked to write focused on having to overcome a challenge in life. I've been fortunate enough to be surrounded by a supportive family and never truly faced what I would consider a hardship. Instead of focusing on financial or familial struggles, which I thought was what the admission board would want to hear, I chose instead to focus on the personal challenge of not being admitted to my dream school, UCLA, right out of high school. Instead of focusing on this set back as a negative, I chose to focus on what I learned from this 'challenge'—to realize the importance of never losing sight of your goals."

—*Heather Gordon, UCLA*

## A Life-Changer

"When I applied to the UCs, the essay topics were pretty much set in stone. One was to describe your world, and the other was to describe something that changed your life. I chose discovering the love of reading for the second one because it really was something that changed my life, and, of course, I thought it would make a great essay."

—*Jessica R. Weinman, UCLA*

## Demonstrating Leadership

"I wrote about gardening, one of my much loved hobbies, and the Community of Character, a local youth group that played a prevalent role in my life. The essay conveying my leadership experience with the COC was an essay topic that came easily to me because of my passion for this organization and the people within it. I started volunteering for this youth group in eighth grade and continued throughout my years in high school. Through public speaking experiences and hosting meetings and events I gained confidence and wanted others to have a similar opportunity to grow. The topic of gardening came to me when I tried to capture my personality. Gardening isn't something that every Orange County student does. This hobby really portrays my calm, sensible personality and it's a hobby that I'm passionate about."

—*Halee Michel, UCLA*

## Connections

"For the UC app I wrote about how I developed as a person based on the connections I made with my family, friends and baseball team. For the second UC essay I just modified my Common App personal statement."

—*Jeremy Press, UC Berkeley*

## Childhood Challenges

"Fortunately, I was able to visit and stay at the UC Berkeley campus a few months before having to apply. During my stay I was able to get a sense of what the campus community and missions/goals were in addition to the undergraduates that were hosting my stay through their student organization. My mentor from my stay at Cal also helped me with my personal statement. Through his encouragement and patience, I considered diverse experiences that helped me to develop as an individual and how it related back to my community. After brainstorming for some days, I decided to write about the challenges I faced since I was little and how they have shaped the world I live in. For one of the essays, I wrote about developing my multilingual and communication skills within my family and local community, and how those skills helped me to break down barriers between those different from me."

*—Anonymous, UC Berkeley*

## Drawing on Two Experiences

"The first question asks to describe the world I've grown up in, such as my family, community or school, and describe how that's changed my goals. For this essay, I had the explicit notion to write about my family. Growing up as a first generation student to have the opportunity to go to college, I wanted to illustrate my upbringing in a conflicted household who had different views on pursuing higher education. I didn't give this topic much thought—it was obvious to me how much family impacted my perspective on college, so I wrote from my experiences at home.

"The second essay asks to describe a personal contribution that's important to me and explain why this makes me proud or relates to the person I am. This prompt was open-ended in my eyes and took me a while to pinpoint a specific contribution I could zero in on and write about. Finally, I came to the decision to write about a health internship I've acquired during my high school career. I chose this specific topic because it allowed me to write about my fear of public speaking, and my reason behind my choosing a health internship."

*—Carol Nguyen, UC Berkeley*

## A Last-Minute Topic

"The topic I chose related to growing out of being a wallflower. I had a really hard time picking this topic because at the time, I was really uncomfortable writing about myself, so to be honest, I picked it at the last minute."

*—Christine Luc, UC Irvine*

## My Favorite Job

"I wrote about my experience teaching dance classes to young children. This was my job throughout high school and it was such a rewarding experience. It was also a tough job and taught me patience, leadership and dealing with angry parents! To this day, being a dance teacher was my favorite job I've ever had and helped me decide that I do want to go back into teaching in the future."

*—Christina Wiesendanger, UC Santa Barbara*

## Change from a Trip

"The theme for my personal statement revolved around a trip I took during my junior year of high school, Sojourn to the Past. Sojourn is a ten-day journey that takes students into the deep South to learn about the civil rights movement and hear first-person accounts from many survivors of the movement still living today. This journey had a profound impact on the way I viewed others around me. Following this ten-day trip, I became more aware of injustices occurring around me, both on a large and small scale.

"For my essay, I wrote about my interactions with a classmate named Sophia.* She was a girl with whom I had had very little contact before the trip, but I had friends who had made their distaste of her clearly visible. They derided her and were not very nice to her, and when this had occurred, I had either turned the other way or had ignored it. However, after Sojourn, I realized I could no longer be a silent witness to her mistreatment. I came to value the idea of not being a bystander to injustice, and began to make the effort to accept her, be kind towards her and stand up for her when she was the victim of my friends' mockery. I wove in lessons I had learned on Sojourn and how I attempted to apply them to events in my life."

—*Anonymous, UC Berkeley*

\* Name has been changed.

## Struggles and Rewards

"I selected my experience as a Polynesian dance teacher because I believe that it portrays a lot about the kind of person I am and what my goals are. My role as a dance teacher involves the struggles I face as well as how rewarding it is because I am able to work with children and help them in discovering their passions which is something I really enjoy and would like to incorporate into my future career."

—*Kaitlyn Makanaakua Basnett, Accepted by UC Irvine, UCLA and UC San Diego*

## Looking Inward

"My first topic was my interest in film-making, and my second topic was my leadership position in a community service club. I chose these because they were specific to who I was at the moment. Following film represented my desire to do what I wanted to do without influence from societal factors or even my family. My rise in a leadership position represented my desire to be a leader as well as help out the community."

—*Armand Nelson Zenarosa Cuevas, UC Berkeley*

## Tricking Myself into Getting Comfortable

"Here are a few of the topics/features I remember about my essay: I wrote the essay in a third-person limited narrative. I've always considered myself a modest person so boasting and emphasizing my accomplishments didn't feel very comfortable for me. I think by writing in the third-person, it helped me express my thoughts by subtly tricking me into thinking I was talking about someone else. Although I don't know for certain, I think it also separated my essay a bit than the others that are written in first-person."

*—Kris Thomson, UC Berkeley*

## Motivations

"For the open-ended essay topic, I discussed why I chose my field of study and why I was applying to the UC system rather than the CSU system. I knew the reviewer would want to know what motivated me, as it would determine how I made it through my schooling and what I would do with my education after college."

*—Stephanie Anderson, UCLA*

## Drawing on Experiences

"I chose to write about some of my family background and my experiences as a cross country captain for these essays. I chose to write about cross country because it was an important experience, and about my family background because I thought it interesting."

*—Edward Shafron, UCLA*

## A Real Impact

"I wrote about what it was like growing up as the youngest of five brothers and how that helped shape my character and world view. I remember (all those years ago...) trying to figure out what to write about and seeing all of my friends grappling with the same problem. All of the "good" sample essays that we read usually talked about some form of overcoming adversity. I am very fortunate in my life and had not faced too much adversity as a high school senior applying to college. Many of my friends found themselves in the same boat, but attempted to write a "sob story" essay anyways—it always came across as disingenuous to me. So, when it came time to sit down and write mine, I thought that I could write about my experience growing up as the youngest of five brothers, since I felt that it was something that had really impacted upon my growth and development. It also gave me a chance to give my essay some levity, humor and personality, which I felt was something often overlooked in my many of my peers' essays."

*—Josh Klaristenfeld, UC Berkeley*

## Leadership

"Each UC has a specific quality that they are looking for students to accentuate, and UCLA's quality is leadership. Now that doesn't necessarily meant that you need to be involved in leadership, be the team captain, etc. but it does mean that in whatever activity you do, you need to show how you have gained leadership qualities. For example, in one of my essays I wrote about my family's annual vacation to Bass Lake. I told a specific (specifics are always good, don't be too general in your essays) story about a time when my cousin got pretty badly injured while wake boarding and I stepped up to the plate and directed each of my family members with what to do and how to take care of him in a safe and timely manner. That story is a great example of a college essay (not to toot my own horn haha) because it involves my family, traditions, wake boarding (which is a sport I am passionate about) and my ability to take charge, especially in emergency situations. These are all great qualities of an essay, but they are especially good because they tell the reader about who I really am.

"That is my next tip, stay true to yourself, that's why my essay turned out well, because it was true, and it was something that I truly cared about. I always encourage my friends who are applying to colleges to truly take the time to think about something (an activity, an experience, a tradition, even a single moment in time) that makes you want to write your essay. Something that brings out the passion that you have, no matter what the thing is."

—*Amber Fearon, UCLA*

# 18

# ADVICE ON WRITING FROM UNIVERSITY OF CALIFORNIA STUDENTS

### Being Honest

"My advice is to be honest in your essay. Your true voice and personality will resonate much stronger with your reader than a feigned point of view that spells out exactly what you think the reader wants to hear.

"Be sure to run your essays by anyone who will read them—teachers, parents, friends, etc. In addition for proofreading for grammar and spelling, they can also offer an outside point of view and could remind you of important points that might have been forgotten.

"Remember to enjoy the process! Yes, applying for school is a lot of hard work, but college is going to be a fun and exciting time. Really make sure you are taking it all in and making the most of the process.

"You will be asked to write multiple essays (on top of what is probably a very busy school, social life and extra-curricular schedule). Make sure that you are planning ample time to write and refine each essay—ideally one essay a week. Think about splitting yourself into two people: the writer and the editor. These two people should never sit down to work at the same time. Write the essay in full in one day without making any edits. Then, a few days later, come back to essay with your most critical eye to clarify concepts and refine the overall message."

—*Heather Gordon, UCLA*

## Writing the Essay for You

"In order to create a strong essay, I would recommend that the essay isn't written with the intent to get into college but rather for yourself. This way you can pour your soul into it while being authentic and genuine. By the end, your essay will be so incredibly important and meaningful that anyone who has the honor to read it, will be amazed by your maturity, vulnerability, determination, talents and ultimately by *you*."

—*Catherine Bronzo, UCLA*

## Standing Out

"My best piece of advice for anyone writing an admissions essay is to find something that makes you stand out as an individual. Each school is receiving thousands of applications with scores and grades as good as yours, or better. I have met several students at UCLA who, although they had worse scores and grades than mine, had a more interesting story to tell. Talk about what makes you different or what hardship you have overcome. Also try to make it interesting; no one likes to read a boring essay. If your writing sounds monotonous in your head, edit it until it works. Read it out loud and have other people read it and give you feedback, especially college counselors and teachers."

—*Jessica R. Weinman, UCLA*

## Caring about the Topic

"I'd say to express who you are and what you honestly care about. Don't try to make something up and don't write about a topic that you're not fervent about. This is a lot easier said than done, but honestly when you get down to who you are, it's a lot easier to discuss topics that you're passionate about. You need to make yourself slightly vulnerable. They may like it, they may not, but write something that talks to you. It's okay to boast a little!"

—*Halee Michel, UCLA*

## Natural Inspiration

"The best advice I could give is to try to let your ideas come naturally at first. I found my best ideas not when I was sitting at my desk trying to write but just thinking about my surroundings and life during my day. I also talked to my friends a lot during this time about more reflective topics like high school in general, and leaving home."

—*Jeremy Press, UC Berkeley*

## Always Reading and Writing

"My advice: Never stop reading and writing. Write with pen on paper, and read from books. Celebrate your humanity and appreciate God's creation. Technology should not lead to academic decadence."

*—Danish Qasim, UC Berkeley*

## Starting Early

"My best piece of advice is to start writing as soon as the prompt is available. The earlier you start, the more time you have to improve your essay. Also, ask your English teachers to help look over your essay."

*—Daniel Hien Vuong, UC Riverside*

## A Story for Everyone

"Everyone has a story to tell whether it is about adversities you have faced, a major turning point in your life, an experience that changed your perspective, or an interest you are passionate about, that moves you, to contribute your efforts towards to make an impact. Whatever your story is, choose one that you feel most strongly about and tell it in a way that separates you from the thousands of other applicants. It is not good to write an admissions essay in a manner that comes off as whiny, a complaint or pitiful. Claim your story and talk about the challenges and positivity it brought to your life, how you have moved forward and how you will utilize and apply what you have learned to impact your community or for the greater good. In other words talk about perseverance because the admissions committee wants to know you are able to handle and persevere through challenges that you may face in college. Give the readers something to remember you by."

*—Anonymous, UC Berkeley*

## What You Enjoy

"My best piece of advice for a high school senior writing their essay is to most definitely write from the heart. Don't aim to please, rather, write from what you're passionate about and let your intuition guide you from there. Thinking too much about the prompt might make your essay sound generic—avoid this at all costs, please! UC essay readers go through countless numbers of essays—as long as you write genuinely and what you enjoy, your essay will go noticed, and standing out in the application process is crucial, in my opinion."

*—Carol Nguyen, UC Berkeley*

## Writing about Yourself

"It's important to practice learning how to write about yourself, so the sooner you get comfortable with it, the better. In your future, you'll face writing cover letters and essays for graduate school, or you'll get into a field where you'll have to represent a brand as a marketer and vouch for that. This is an important skill to have and it will help you communicate as a person, so don't get hung up on finding it vain or thinking that your self-esteem is too low to do anything like this. Be honest about your strengths and learn to articulate them in a succinct manner."

—Christine Luc, UC Irvine

### Writing about What You Love

"Stand out. I know this is the advice everyone gives, but really dig deep and think about something that you're very passionate about. If you choose a topic that you are not passionate about, it will show and your essay will just get lost among the others. Write about what you love, but try to give it a unique angle that you don't think other people will have."

—Christina Wiesendanger, UC Santa Barbara

### Let Your Topic Evolve

"The best piece of advice I can offer a senior currently writing his or her admissions essay is not to be afraid to change or let the topic of the essay evolve as he or she gets further into the writing process. When I began brain-storming for my essay, the ideas and themes I believed I would write about were noticeably different from the ones about which I actually wrote; this was the product of constant tweaking throughout my writing process. I was worried at the beginning that if I began to write about ideas that were only tangentially related to my main theme, I would mess up my whole essay. But despite these initial reservations, I came to realize that it was okay to let the course of my essay change shape as I worked through draft after draft of my essay. The end product ended up being something different than what I had anticipated, yet I was pleased with the final result."

—Anonymous, UC Berkeley

### The True You

"My best piece of advice would be to write from your heart and show colleges who you really are. If you try and exaggerate or use fancy vocabulary you are not comfortable with, it will prevent the person reading your essay from gaining a sense of who you are as a person as well as prevent you from portraying a real image of yourself."

—Kaitlyn Makanaakua Basnett, Accepted by UC Irvine, UCLA and UC San Diego

### Being Specific

"Pick something very specific and expand on it, even if it seems too personal or too braggy."

—Armand Nelson Zenarosa Cuevas, UC Berkeley

## Explaining Your Transcript

"When writing the essay, think of it as an opportunity to explain anything on your transcript that needs further clarification. Nobody's perfect so using the essay to explain/defend yourself isn't the end of the world. For example, my English scores were lower than my math/science grades. I used the essay to emphasize that although I was challenged in these courses and I did feel like I was growing as a writer, I was never truly enthusiastic about English. Physics and science were always more interesting to me and so I would naturally devote more time and energy studying those.

"Universities are looking for leaders not followers. Everyone's had some leadership responsibilities at some point (big or small). Talking about those sorts of experiences made it pretty easy to boast about myself. Simple things like starting a club or having people look up to you in a certain class/sport are not as trivial as I initially thought."

—*Kris Thomson, UC Berkeley*

## Answering the Prompt

"Make sure to answer the prompt! Don't just talk about your qualities; discuss how those qualities will contribute to your success, the university and the part of the world you want to impact most."

—*Stephanie Anderson, UCLA*

## Testing Out Multiple Essays

"Test out multiple essays, because sometimes what may be a great idea doesn't turn into a great essay. Don't ever feel stuck with what you started with. The application readers will never know how many drafts you deleted before your final product.

"The next tip is a given. Start early. Seriously.

"Next tip. Edit it again and again, have as many people read it as possible, take all of their opinions but don't feel like you have to listen to all of them. This is *your* essay, do with it what you please, but keep in mind that you want the application reader to like it too!

"My college advisor told me that you should always start your essay off with a zinger. A statement that will actually catch the reader's attention. Interest them, be the essay that stands out in their long day, the one they tell their spouse about! This is also where the passion part comes in. If you love what you're writing about, chances are they will too.

"About the content of your essay, maybe you've started out with a personal story. Don't just write about that, everyone has great stories to tell! You have to stand out by relating that story to your personality traits, to your outside activities, to potential things you want to accomplish in the future (maybe at their college...). Make your story mean something by not only telling it, but giving it a moral, a lesson learned, etc.

"Also, there is an optional third essay! Not many people know about it or utilize it. If you have more to say that you didn't put into your other essays or application, then you should write a short third essay. Make sure you're not repeating your other essays otherwise this essay could hurt you, but if you feel like it is something truly important that you do or about yourself then definitely add it in. But keep it short!"

—Amber Fearon, UCLA

## Focus on Writing Style

"The best piece of advice for writing a college essay would be to use a writing style that is unique and interesting."

—Edward Shafron, UCLA

## Getting Personal

"I would recommend choosing a topic that carries personal weight to the writer. I think that it's really easy for a professional admissions officer, who is reading thousands of these essays, to easily spot phony-ness. However, when the applicant can write on a topic that is actually meaningful and can imbue the essay with elements of his or her own personality, then it stands out among that massive pile of applications sitting on the admissions officer's desk. Ultimately, I believe that's the purpose of the college admissions essay, especially for the UC schools. The essay is your chance to bring a human face and personality to the standard application."

—Josh Klaristenfeld, UC Berkeley

# 19

# WHAT I LEARNED FROM WRITING THE ESSAY

**Seeing the Words on the Screen**

"I learned a lot from writing my UC essays, believe it or not. I think it's always difficult to write about myself, because honestly, when do we ever reflect on our hardships and how far we've come? Reading my essay and seeing the actual words on the screen that reflect who I am as a first generation college student says a lot about me and made me more aware of my accomplishments and puts into perspective what I need to do to achieve my long-term goals."

—*Carol Nguyen, UC Berkeley*

**Perceiving Myself Differently**

"After writing it, editing it, rewriting it, trashing it and repeating this about three times—I was finally able to step back and read my final product. It made me realize that no matter what any college thought of my essay or me, I was proud of myself. The essay helped bring a rollercoaster of moments and emotions in my life together, and once I was able to actually read about my own life, I perceived who I was differently, yet positively. I learned that I cannot

**177**

only do anything but everything, and that all my dreams are attainable because I can truthfully overcome any hurdle."

—*Catherine Bronzo, UCLA*

## Perseverance

"This relates more to the application process as a whole, more than the essay itself, but what I ultimately learned about myself is that perseverance is key to achieving any goal.

Since the age of 12, my dream was to graduate from UCLA. I worked very hard in high school, had strong SAT scores, but for whatever reason, the cards did not align and I was denied admission. I had the option to go to other colleges, but I chose to hold true to my dreams and opted to go to community college instead and then transfer to UCLA. It might not have been a direct path, but I was happy to achieve my goal."

—*Heather Gordon, UCLA*

## Defining Differences from Family

"From writing the essay about my world, I learned more about myself. Since I had to find examples of how I was different from my family for my essay, and put those differences into words, I definitely felt even more like an outsider for a while after writing the essay. Most of this was in my head. The religion part is pretty much ignored and the career part has become irrelevant, as I do plan on going to law school after all."

—*Jessica R. Weinman, UCLA*

## Importance of Service and Feelings

"From writing the Community of Character essay I reflected on the importance of the Community of Character in my life. I learned that community service brings me happiness and it's something that I will continue for, well, hopefully as long as I can. Through my gardening essay I truly learned that I am a person of feelings. I really take the world in through my senses and I find an inner peace when working with nature."

—*Halee Michel, UCLA*

## Writing and Editing Style

"I learned a lot about myself when writing the essay and especially while editing. I learned about my style as a writer and a lot of things I need to work on, such as comma usage (still haven't mastered that one) and also what I'm truly passionate about."

—*Shelby Newallis, UCSD*

## An Objective View

"I think I learned a lot about my essay. It is really hard to look at yourself objectively or put any kind of a label or a description of yourself, but when you do it, it makes you feel more confident about who you are."

*—Jeremy Press, UC Berkeley*

## Taking It in

"When one has to write about himself or herself, I believe that they learn some things about themselves that they weren't conscious about in the first place. In the world we live in today, things are always rushed and people often forget stop and take it in for a moment. These essays required me to take a step back and think about who I am, what I want to do with my life and how I can achieve it."

*—Daniel Hien Vuong, UC Riverside*

## Facing Adversities

"During the process of writing my personal statement, I realized I had a young mind and body that had gone through some of the most difficult experiences anyone could go through. For several years, it was a battle to come to terms, accept, and cope with the reality of those experiences. Writing the essays helped me to realize for once in my life, I was proud of the adversities I encountered rather than being consumed by shame, guilt and vulnerability; these three attributes are what bring about change. However, one of the biggest realization was that the power of perspectives can begin to pacify some of the differences between people."

*—Anonymous, UC Berkeley*

## Seeing Growth

"At the time, I learned how far I've come to get to that point. I grew a lot, and I've grown since!"

*—Christine Luc, UC Irvine*

## Career Focus

"Writing my essay helped me realize how passionate I am about teaching and where I want it to take me in the future."

*—Christina Wiesendanger, UC Santa Barbara*

## Portraying Myself

"I really tried to show who I am as a person through my writing, and translating myself into an essay helped me to gain an understanding of how I wanted to portray myself and my interest to colleges."

*—Kaitlyn Makanaakua Basnett, Accepted by UC Irvine, UCLA and UC San Diego*

## Taking Pride

"I learned to take pride in such qualities about myself and not be ashamed for following a career that wasn't stable, or doing a leadership position in merely community services versus business, student council or something more highly regarded."

—*Armand Nelson Zenarosa Cuevas, UC Berkeley*

## Reinforcing What I Already Knew

"I can't think of anything that I really learned about myself. I think writing the essay only reinforced what I knew—I wanted to expand my knowledge in the field of math and science (specifically engineering)."

—*Kris Thomson, UC Berkeley*

## Defining Myself

"I think writing these essays helped define myself and my experiences better."

—*Edward Shafron, UCLA*

## Thinking about Family Relationships

"I went through a whole bunch of ideas for my college essay before eventually picking one that I felt comfortable writing about. Thinking about writing an essay about growing up as the youngest of five brothers forced me to consider my relationships with each of them (as well as my parents). It made me realize the extent to which my character and outlook was shaped by that experience."

—*Josh Klaristenfeld, UC Berkeley*

## Cranking out Drafts

"As I wrote the essay, I was able to explore my abilities as a write a familiarize myself with the methods and conventions I found helpful when writing. For example, while many of my friends mentioned they would do a draft of their essay every few days, let it sit, and then come back and revise it, I discovered that the most successful method for me was just sitting down for a few hours and cranking out multiple drafts, which I would immediately add to or edit. Thus, much of my essay-writing process also helped me to assess my abilities and strengths as a writer."

—*Anonymous, UC Berkeley*

Some of the students in this book were accepted by University of California schools but attended other universities.

## Stanford University

Kaitlyn Makanaakua Basnett
Jackie Botts
Ali Cardenas
Inès C. Gérard-Ursin
Ben L.
Cristina H. Mezgravis
Nhi Yen Nguyen
Sumaya Quillian
Hayley Ritterhern
Brian Tashjian

## Willamette University

Mitchell Brisacher

# ABOUT THE AUTHORS

HARVARD GRADUATES GEN AND KELLY TANABE are the founders of SuperCollege and the award-winning authors of fourteen books including *The Ultimate Scholarship Book*, *The Ultimate Guide to America's Best Colleges*, *50 Successful Ivy League Application Essays*, *Accepted! 50 Successful College Admission Essays* and *1001 Ways to Pay for College*.

Together, Gen and Kelly were accepted to every school to which they applied, including all of the Ivy League colleges and Stanford, and won more than $100,000 in merit-based scholarships. They were able to leave Harvard debt-free and their parents guilt-free.

Gen and Kelly give workshops at high schools across the country. They have made hundreds of appearances on television and radio and have served as expert sources for respected publications including *U.S. News & World Report*, *USA Today*, *The New York Times*, *Chicago Sun-Times*, *New York Daily News*, *Chronicle of Higher Education* and *Seventeen*.

Gen grew up in Waialua, Hawaii. Between eating banana-flavored shave ice and basking in the sun, he was president of the Student Council, captain of the speech team and a member of the tennis team. A graduate of Waialua High School, he was the first student from his school to be accepted at Harvard. In college, Gen was chair of the Eliot House Committee and graduated magna cum laude with a degree in both History and East Asian Studies.

Kelly attended Whitney High School, a nationally ranked public high school in her hometown of Cerritos, California. She was the editor of the school newspaper, assistant editor of the yearbook and founder of a public service club to promote literacy. In college, she was the co-director of the HAND public service program and the brave co-leader of a Brownie Troop. She graduated magna cum laude with a degree in Sociology.

Gen, Kelly, their sons Zane and Kane and their dog Sushi live in Belmont, California.